DEPARTMENT OF THE NAVY
HEADQUARTERS UNITED STATES MARINE CORPS
3000 MARINE CORPS PENTAGON
WASHINGTON, DC 20350-3000

UC-35C/D T&R MANUAL

DEPARTMENT OF THE NAVY
HEADQUARTERS UNITED STATES MARINE CORPS
3000 MARINE CORPS PENTAGON
WASHINGTON, DC 20350-3000

NAVMC 3500.92
C 4610
I 8 NOV 2010

NAVMC 3500.92

From: Commandant of the Marine Corps
To: Distribution List

Subj: UC-35C/D T&R MANUAL

Ref: (a) NAVMC 3500.14B

Encl: (1) UC-35C/D T&R MANUAL

1. <u>Purpose</u>. To revise standards and regulations regarding the training of UC-35C/D aircrew per the reference.

2. <u>Information</u>. Highlights of major training and readiness planning considerations included in this publication are as follows:

    a. Mission Essential Task (MET) incorporation.

    b. Addition of Aviation Career Progression Model (ACPM) curriculum.

    c. Emphasis on Mission Skills versus Core Skills.

    d. Re-naming and re-numbering of Phases from 3 digit to 4 digit codes.

    e. Standardized NATOPS and instrument evaluation policy.

3. <u>Recommendations</u>. Recommended changes to this Manual are invited, and may be submitted via the syllabus sponsor and the appropriate chain of command to: Commanding General, Training and Education Command, Aviation Training Division using standard Naval correspondence or the Automated Message Handling System plain language address: CG TECOM ATD.

4. <u>Reserve Applicability</u>. This Manual is applicable to the Marine Corps Total Force.

5. <u>Certification</u>. Reviewed and approved this date.

R. C. FOX
By direction

DISTRIBUTION: 10039181300

CHAPTER 1

UC-35C/D TRAINING AND READINESS UNIT REQUIREMENTS

CHAPTER 1

UC-35C/D

100. **MARINE OPERATIONAL SUPPORT AIRCRAFT (OSA) SQUADRONS AND DETACHMENTS (VMR-1 and VMR Det. UC-35C/D) UNIT TRAINING AND READINESS REQUIREMENTS.** The goal of Marine Aviation is to attain and maintain combat readiness to support Expeditionary Maneuver Warfare while conserving resources. The standards established in this program are validated by subject matter experts to maximize combat capabilities for assigned METs. These standards describe and define unit capabilities and requirements necessary to maintain proficiency in mission skills and combat leadership. Training events are based on specific requirements and performance standards to ensure a common base of training and depth of combat capability.

101. **OSA/UC-35C/D MISSION.** Provide time-sensitive air transport of high priority passengers and cargo to, within, and between theaters of war.

102. **TABLE OF ORGANIZATION (T/O).** As of this publication date, UC-35 VMR-1 and VMR Dets for both the Active and Reserve Forces are authorized:

Table of Organization Active Forces		
VMR-1 MCAS Cherry Point	VMR Det MCAS Miramar	VMR Det MCAS Futenma
T/O # 02207	T/O # M02209	T/O # M02204
2 UC-35D	2 UC-35D	3 UC-35D
Pilots	Pilots	Pilots
3	6	6
Transport Aircrewman	Transport Aircrewman	Transport Aircrewman
3	2	2
Table of Organization Reserve Forces		
VMR JRB Belle Chase		VMR NAF Andrews
T/O M01129		T/O M04801
2 UC-35C		3 UC-35D
Pilots		Pilots
21		21
Transport Aircrewman		Transport Aircrewman
5		5
Table of Organization (Deployed Detachment)		
2 UC-35C/D		1 UC-35C/D
Pilots		Pilots
7		5
Transport Aircrewman		Transport Aircrewman
3*		2*
*The Transport Aircrewman is not required on all Mission Flights		

103. <u>CORE SKILLS AND MISSION SKILL ABBREVIATIONS</u>. Shading indicates Core Plus Skills.

CORE SKILLS	
CACT	COMMAND AIRCRAFT CREWTRAINING
FAM	FAMILIARIZATION
NFAM	NIGHT FAMILIARIZATION
INST	INSTRUMENT
CP	CO-PILOT PROCEDURES
MISSION SKILLS	
OSA	OPERATIONAL SUPPORT AIRLIFT
ALS	AIR LOGISTICS SUPPORT
CORE PLUS SKILLS	
ASE	AIRCRAFT SURVIVABILITY EQUIPMENT
INT PROC	INTERNATIONAL PROCEDURES
MISSION PLUS	
AS	ASSAULT SUPPORT
EXP	EXPEDITIONARY SHORE-BASED OPERATIONS

104. <u>CORE METL AND CORE METL OUTPUT STANDARDS</u>

1. <u>Core METL</u>. A list of specified tasks that VMR-1 and VMR Dets are designed to perform.

Core METL
MCT 1.3.4.1.2	Conduct Operational Support Airlift
MCT 4.3.8	Conduct Air Logistics Support

Core Plus
MCT 1.3.4	Conduct Assault Support Operations
MCT 1.3.3.3.2	Conduct Aviation Operations From Expeditionary Shore-Based Sites

2. <u>VMR-1 or VMR Det</u>. The required level of performance that VMR-1 or a VMR Det must be capable of sustaining to be considered MET-Ready.

VMR-1 or VMR Det (UC-35C/D)				
Core METL Output Standards (3/2 A/C)				
MCT	MET	MAXIMUM DAILY SORTIES	MAXIMUM SORTIES PER MET	CMMR
MCT 1.3.4.1.2 OSA	Conduct Operational Support Airlift	9/6	9/6	4/3
MCT 4.3.8 ALS	Conduct Air Logistics Support		9/6	4/3
Core Plus METL Output Standards				
MCT	MET	MAXIMUM DAILY SORTIES	MAXIMUM SORTIES PER MET	CMMR
MCT 1.3.4 AS	Conduct Assault Support Operations	9/6	9/6	4/3
MCT 1.3.3.3.2 EXP	Conduct Aviation Operations From Expeditionary Shore-Based Sites		9/6	4/3

Note: VMR-1 or a VMR Det (UC-35C/D) (3/2 A/C) is able to execute 9/6 total overall sorties on a daily (24 hour period) basis. Based on historical flight hour data, average sortie duration is 1.7 hours for the UC-35C/D.

3. **VMR Deployed Detachment.** The required level of performance that VMR-1 or a VMR Det must be capable of sustaining during deployed contingency operations to be considered MET-ready.

VMR Deployed Detachment (UC-35C/D)				
Core METL Output Standards (2/1 A/C Det)				
MCT	MET	MAXIMUM DAILY SORTIES	MAXIMUM SORTIES PER MET	CMMR
MCT 1.3.4.1.2 OSA	Conduct Operational Support Airlift	6/3	6/3	3/2
MCT 4.3.8 ALS	Conduct Air Logistics Support		6/3	3/2
Core Plus METL Output Standards				
MCT	MET	MAXIMUM DAILY SORTIES	MAXIMUM SORTIES PER MET	CMMR
MCT 1.3.4 AS	Conduct Assault Support Operations	6/3	6/3	3/2
MCT 1.3.3.3.2 EXP	Conduct Aviation Operations From Expeditionary Shore-Based Sites		6/3	3/2

Note: A VMR UC-35C/D Deployed Detachment (2/1 A/C) is able to execute 6/3 total overall sorties on a daily (24 hour period) basis during contingency/combat operations. Based on historical flight hour data, average sortie duration is 1.7 hours for the UC-35C/D.

105. **CORE MCT TO CORE/MISSION/CORE PLUS SKILL MATRIX.** Provides a pictorial view of the relationship between the Core MCT (Marine Corps Task) and each Core/Mission/Core Plus skill required to perform the MCT. Shading indicates a Core Plus.

UC-35C/D											
Mission Essential Task To Core/Mission/Core Plus Skill Matrix											
MISSION ESSENTIAL TASK (MET) // MARINE CORPS TASK (MCT)	CORE SKILLS 2000 PHASE					MISSION SKILLS 3000 PHASE		CORE PLUS 4000 PHASE			
	FAM	INST	NFAM	CP	FAM REV	OSA	ALS	ASE	INT PROC	AS	EXP
MCT 1.3.4.1.2 Conduct Operational Support Airlift OSA	X	X	X	X	X	X		X			
MCT 4.3.8 Conduct Air Logistics Support ALS	X	X	X	X	X		X	X			
CORE PLUS											
MCT 1.3.4 Conduct Assault Support Operations AS	X	X	X	X	X			X	X	X	
MCT 1.3.3.3.2 Conduct Aviation Operations From Expeditionary Shore-Based Sites EXP	X	X	X					X			X

106. CMMR CORE/MISSION/CORE PLUS SKILLS CREW DEFINITION AND PROFICIENCY
REQUIREMENTS

    a. VMR-1 or VMR Det. This table delineates crew position and
proficiency requirements for each Core/Mission/Core Plus Skill. The numbers
associated with each crew position column reflect the number of
Core/Mission/Core Plus Skill proficient individuals required.

VMR-1 or VMR Det (UC-35C/D)			
CMMR (3/2 A/C)			
CORE SKILLS (2000 Phase)			
CORE SKILL	PILOTS	TRANSPORT AIRCREWMAN	CREWS
FAM	17/11	3/2	4/3
INST	17/11	N/A	4/3
NFAM	17/11	N/A	4/3
CP	17/11	N/A	4/3
FAM REV	17/11	N/A	4/3
MISSION SKILLS (3000 Phase)			
MISSION SKILL	PILOTS	TRANSPORT AIRCREWMAN	CREWS
OSA	17/11	3/2	4/3
ALS	17/11	3/2	4/3
CORE PLUS (4000 Phase)			
CORE PLUS SKILL	PILOTS	TRANSPORT AIRCREWMAN	CREWS
INTL PROC	7/5	3/2	3/2
ASE	7/5	3/2	3/2
MISSION PLUS	PILOTS	TRANSPORT AIRCREWMAN	CREWS
AS	7/5	3/2	3/2
EXP	7/5	3/2	3/2
*The Transport Aircrewman is not required on all Mission Flights			

    b. VMR Deployed Detachment. This table delineates crew position and
proficiency requirements for each Core/Mission/Core Plus Skill. The numbers
associated with each crew position column reflect the number of
Core/Mission/Core Plus Skill proficient individuals required.

VMR Deployed Detachment (UC-35C/D)			
CMMR (2/1 A/C)			
CORE SKILLS (2000 Phase)			
CORE SKILL	PILOTS	TRANSPORT AIRCREWMAN	CREWS
FAM	7/5	2/1*	3/2
INST	7/5	N/A	3/2
NFAM	7/5	N/A	3/2
CP	7/5	N/A	3/2
FAM REV	7/5	N/A	3/2
MISSION SKILLS (3000 Phase)			
MISSION SKILL	PILOTS	TRANSPORT AIRCREWMAN	CREWS
OSA	7/5	2/1*	3/2
ALS	7/5	2/1*	3/2
CORE PLUS (4000 Phase)			
CORE PLUS SKILL	PILOTS	TRANSPORT AIRCREWMAN	CREWS
INTL PROC	5/4	2/1*	2/2
ASE	5/4	2/1*	2/2
MISSION PLUS	PILOTS	TRANSPORT AIRCREWMAN	CREWS
AS	5/4	2/1*	2/2
EXP	5/4	2/1*	2/2
*The Transport Aircrewman is not required on all Mission Flights			

107. INSTRUCTOR REQUIREMENTS

    a. VMR-1 or VMR Det. VMR-1 or VMR Det should possess the following numbers of personnel with the instructor designations listed in the matrix.

VMR-1 or VMR Det (UC-35C/D) CMMR (3/2 A/C)		
INSTRUCTOR DESIGNATIONS (5000 PHASE)		
DESIGNATIONS	PILOTS	TRANSPORT AIRCREWMAN
ANI (Assistant NATOPS Inst)	3/2	1/1
NI (NATOPS Instructor)	1/1	1/1
Instrument Evaluator	3/2	N/A
Transport Aircrewman Instructor	N/A	3/2

    b. VMR Deployed Detachment. A deployed VMR Det should possess the following numbers of personnel with the instructor designations listed in the matrix.

VMR Deployed Det (UC-35C/D) CMMR (2/1 A/C)		
INSTRUCTOR DESIGNATIONS (5000 PHASE)		
DESIGNATIONS	PILOTS	TRANSPORT AIRCREWMAN
ANI (Assistant NATOPS Inst)	2/1	1/1
NI (NATOPS Instructor)	1/1	1/1
Instrument Evaluator	1/1	N/A
Transport Aircrewman Instructor	N/A	1/1

108. CMMR FLIGHT LEADERSHIP REQUIREMENTS

    a. VMR-1 or VMR Det. VMR-1 or a VMR Det to be considered Core Competent must possess the following numbers of crews with the listed flight leadership designations.

VMR-1 or VMR Det (UC-35C/D) CMMR (3/2 A/C)		
FLIGHT LEADERSHIP (6000 PHASE)		
DESIGNATION	PILOTS	TRANSPORT AIRCREWMAN
T3P	3/2	N/A
T2P	3/2	N/A
TAC	6/5	N/A
TRANSPORT AIRCREWMAN	N/A	3/2
FCF	3/2	N/A

    b. VMR Deployed Detachment. A deployed VMR Detachment should possess the following numbers of personnel with the flight leadership designations.

VMR Deployed Det (UC-35C/D) CMMR (2/1 A/C)		
FLIGHT LEADERSHIP (6000 PHASE)		
DESIGNATION	PILOTS	TRANSPORT AIRCREWMAN
T3P	0/0	N/A
T2P	2/1	N/A
TAC	5/4	N/A
TRANSPORT AIRCREWMAN	N/A	2/1
FCF	1/1	N/A

CHAPTER 2

UC-35C/D PILOT/7554

CHAPTER 2

UC-35 PILOT/7554

200. <u>UC-35 PILOT/7554 INDIVIDUAL TRAINING AND READINESS REQUIREMENTS</u>. This T&R syllabus is based on specific goals and performance standards designed to ensure individual proficiency in Core, Mission and Core Plus Skills. The goal of this chapter is to develop individual and unit war fighting capabilities.

201. <u>UC-35 PILOT TRAINING PROGRESSION MODEL</u>. This model represents the recommended training progression for the average UC-35 pilot crewmember. Units should use the model as a guide to generate individual training plans.

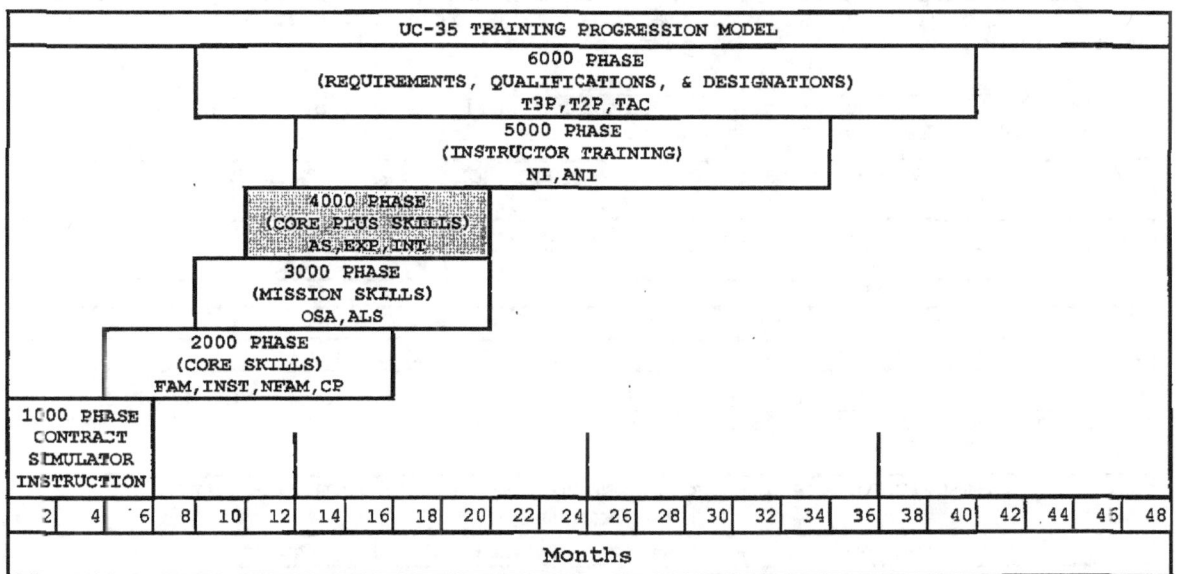

202. <u>INDIVIDUAL CORE SKILL PROFICIENCY (CSP) REQUIREMENTS</u>. A CSP crew consists of individuals representing each crew position who have achieved and currently maintain individual CSP. In order to be considered proficient in a Core Skill, an individual must attain and maintain proficiency in Core Skill events as delineated in the below paragraphs.

1. <u>Events Required to Attain Individual CSP</u>. To initially attain CSP in a Core Skill, an individual must simultaneously have a proficient status in all of the Core Skill (2000 Phase) T&R events listed in the table below for that Core Skill.

INDIVIDUAL CORE SKILL PROFICIENCY (CSP) ATTAIN TABLE UC-35C/D Pilot				
FAM	**INST**	**NFAM**	**CP**	**FAM REV**
2100 2101R	2200R 2201R	2300R	2400 2401R	2500
Gray highlight & an R suffix on the event code = Refresher POI				
An S prefix on the event code = Event conducted in a simulator				

2. <u>Events Required to Maintain Individual CSP</u>. To maintain CSP in a Core Skill, an individual must maintain proficiency in all 2000 phase T&R events listed for that Core Skill:

INDIVIDUAL CORE SKILL PROFICIENCY (CSP) MAINTAIN TABLE UC-35C/D Pilot				
FAM	**INST**	**NFAM**	**CP**	**FAM REV**
2101R	2201R	2300R	2401R	
Gray highlight & an R suffix on the event code = Refresher POI				
An S prefix on the event code = Event conducted in a simulator				

203. <u>INDIVIDUAL MISSION SKILL PROFICIENCY (MSP) REQUIREMENTS</u>. A MSP crew consists of individuals representing each crew position who have achieved and currently maintain Individual MSP. To be considered proficient in a Mission Skill, an individual must attain and maintain proficiency in Mission Skill events as delineated in the below paragraphs.

1. <u>Events Required to Attain Individual MSP</u>. To initially attain MSP in a Mission Skill, an individual must simultaneously have a proficient status in all 3000 phase T&R events listed for that Mission Skill:

INDIVIDUAL MISSION SKILL PROFICIENCY (MSP) ATTAIN TABLE UC-35C/D Pilot	
T&R events required to Attain MSP (3000 Phase)	
OSA	**ALS**
3100R	3200R
Gray highlight & an R suffix on the event code = Refresher POI	
An S prefix on the event code = Event conducted in a simulator	

2. <u>Events Required to Maintain Individual MSP</u>. To maintain MSP in a Mission Skill, an individual must maintain proficiency in all 3000 phase T&R events listed for that Mission Skill:

INDIVIDUAL MISSION SKILL PROFICIENCY (MSP) MAINTAIN TABLE UC-35C/D Pilot	
T&R events required to Maintain MSP (3000 Phase)	
OSA	**ALS**
3100R	3200R
Gray highlight & an R suffix on the event code = Refresher POI	
An S prefix on the event code = Event conducted in a simulator	

204. <u>INDIVIDUAL CORE PLUS SKILL/MISSION PLUS SKILL PROFICIENCY REQUIREMENTS</u>

1. <u>Events Required to Attain Individual Proficiency in Core Plus Skills and Mission Plus Skills</u>. Proficiency in Core Plus Skills/Mission Plus Skills is not required to obtain unit CSP. Training to Core Plus Skills/Mission Plus Skills is at the discretion of the unit commanding officer. To initially attain proficiency in a Core Plus Skill/Mission Plus Skill, an individual must simultaneously have a proficient status in all T&R events listed for that Core Plus Skill/Mission Plus Skill.

INDIVIDUAL CORE PLUS SKILL PROFICIENCY ATTAIN TABLE UC-35C/D Pilot		
T&R events required to Attain Core Plus Proficiency (4000 Phase)		
AS	**EXP**	**INT**
4100R	4200R	4300R
		4301R
Gray highlight & an R suffix on the event code = Refresher POI		
An S prefix on the event code = Event conducted in a simulator		

2. Events Required to Maintain Individual Proficiency in Core Plus Skills and Mission Plus Skills. To maintain proficiency in a Core Plus Skill/Mission Plus Skill, an individual must maintain proficiency in all T&R events listed in the table below for that Core Plus Skill Mission Plus Skill:

INDIVIDUAL CORE PLUS SKILL PROFICIENCY MAINTAIN TABLE UC-35C/D Pilot		
T&R events required to Maintain Core Plus Proficiency (4000 Phase)		
AS	EXP	INT
4100R	4200R	4300R
		4301R
Gray highlight & an R suffix on the event code = Refresher POI		
An S prefix on the event code = Event conducted in a simulator		

205. CERTIFICATION, QUALIFICATION AND DESIGNATION TABLES. The tables below delineate T&R events required to be completed to attain proficiency, initial qualifications and designations. In addition to event requirements, all required stage lectures, briefs, squadron training, prerequisites, and other criteria shall be completed prior to completing final events. Certification, qualification and designation letters signed by the commanding officer shall be placed in Aircrew Performance Records (APR) and NATOPS. Loss of proficiency in all qualification events causes the associated qualification to be lost. Regaining a qualification requires completing all R-coded syllabus events associated with that qualification.

INDIVIDUAL DESIGNATION REQUIREMENTS UC-35C/D Pilot	
Designation	Initial Event Designation Requirements
ANI	5100,5101,5102,5103
NI	5100,5101,5102,5103
T3P	6200
T2P	6300,6301
TAC	6400,6401,6402
FCF	6500,6501,6009

INDIVIDUAL QUALIFICATION REQUIREMENTS UC-35C/D Pilot	
Qualification	Initial Event Qualification Requirements
NATOPS	6000,6001,6002,6100
STANDARD INSTRUMENT	6003,6004,6005,6101
SPECIAL INSTRUMENT	6003,6004,6005,6102
CRM	6006,6007,6103

206. PROGRAMS OF INSTRUCTION (POI)

1. General. The time required to train a UC-35C/D Pilot to completion of the Core Plus phase will vary. Assignment to a specific POI is determined by previous Military Fixed-Wing experience and is listed in the UC-35C/D NATOPS Manual. Those aviators with less than 200 military Fixed-Wing hours* shall be assigned to the Basic (B) POI. Those aviators with more than 200 military Fixed-Wing hours* will normally be assigned to the Conversion (C) POI. Those aviators that have been previously designated a UC-35C/D TAC and are returning to a DIFOP status should be assigned to the Refresher(R) POI. When a crewmember completes a stage of training, that crewmember need only maintain proficiency in the R coded events for that stage to remain proficient.

*Note - See UC-35C/D NATOPS Manual for current flight hour requirements.

2. Basic (B) POI. Basic (B) Pilots shall fly the entire syllabus.

WEEKS	COURSE	PERFORMING ACTIVITY
1-8	Core Skill Introduction Training	CACT
9-16	Core Skill Training	VMR Det
16-52	Mission Skill Training	VMR Det
16-52	Core Plus Training	VMR Det

3. Conversion (C) POI. Conversion (C) shall fly those events annotated with a C.

WEEKS	COURSE	PERFORMING ACTIVITY
1-8	Core Skill Introduction Training	CACT
9-16	Core Skill Training	VMR Det
16-52	Mission Skill Training	VMR Det
16-52	Core Plus Training	VMR Det

4. Refresher (R) POI. Refresher Pilots shall fly those events annotated with a R.   Commanding officers/OICs will review the qualifications, previous experience, currency, and demonstrated ability of Refresher Pilots with a view towards combining required flights.

WEEKS	COURSE	PERFORMING ACTIVITY
1-8	Core Skill Introduction Training	CACT
9-12	Core Skill Training	VMR Det
13-26	Mission Skill Training	VMR Det
13-26	Core Plus Training	VMR Det

207. CORE SKILL INTRODCUTION PHASE (1000)

1. General

    a. Core Skill Introduction training for the UC-35C/D is conducted by a Civilian Approved Contracted Training (CACT) facility. The UC-35C/D Syllabus Sponsor is responsible for contract negotiations and syllabus content/changes. Recommendations for CACT changes shall be submitted to the Syllabus Sponsor.

    b. All academic requirements for this phase of training are incorporated into the CACT course.

    c. All events in the Core Skill Introduction phase shall be evaluated and documented by a civilian instructor The Syllabus Sponsor shall ensure standardization of civilian contracted instructors.

    d. Event completion is predicated upon demonstrated proficiency. When an individual successfully accomplishes the requirements of an event per the performance standards, the individual should log completion of the event (enter the appropriate T&R code) in M-SHARP. When the event is entered into M-SHARP, the individual's proficiency date for that event is automatically updated to reflect the date the event was completed. When supervising individual events, unit instructors/leaders shall ensure that trainees demonstrate proficiency per T&R standards prior to logging successful event completion. Evaluating individual proficiency in an event normally requires both objective and subjective assessment. If an individual fails to accomplish the requirements of an event per the performance standards, the individual should not log that event and the proficiency status for that event remains unchanged. Times indicated for each event are for planning purposes only.

   e. Environmental Conditions. Pilots shall fly events annotated with an N at least 30 minutes after official sunset. Events shall be flown in accordance with environmental conditions listed in the matrix below:

ENVIRONMENTAL CONDITIONS	
Code	Meaning
D	Shall be flown during hours of daylight: (by exception - there is no use of a symbol)
N*	Shall be flown during hours of darkness must be flown unaided
(N*)	May be flown during hours of darkness - If flown during hours of darkness must be flown unaided
Note - If the event is to be flown in the simulator the Simulator Instructor shall set the desired environmental conditions for the event.	

2. <u>Civilian Approved Contractor Training (CACT) Ground School</u>

ACAD-1000   55.0   *   B,C   CLRM

   <u>Goal</u>. UC-35C/D Systems Initial.

   <u>Requirements</u>. Per current contract.

   <u>Performance Standard</u>. Per current contract.

ACAD-1001   12.0   365   B,C,R CLRM

   <u>Goal</u>. UC-35C/D Systems Recurrent.

   <u>Requirements</u>. Per current contract.

   <u>Performance Standard</u>. Per current contract.

ACAD-1002   3.0   *   B,C   CLRM

   <u>Goal</u>. RVSM.

   <u>Requirements</u>. Per current contract.

   <u>Performance Standard</u>. Per current contract.

ACAD-1003   2.0   365   B,C,R CLRM

   <u>Goal</u>. Weather Radar.

   <u>Requirements</u>. Per current contract.

   <u>Performance Standard</u>. Per current contract.

ACAD-1004   21.0   *   B,C   CLRM

    Goal. CACT International Procedures Initial.

    Requirements. Per current contract.

    Performance Standard. Per current contract.

ACAD-1005   4.0   365   R   CLRM

    Goal. CACT International Procedures Recurrent.

    Requirements. Per current contract.

    Performance Standard. Per current contract.

    Prerequisite. 1002

4. Civilian Approved Contractor Training (CACT) Simulator Training

CACT-1101   4.0   *   B,C   SIM   S   (N*)

    Goal. Per current contract.

    Requirements. Per current contract.

    Performance Standard. Per current contract.

CACT-1102   4.0   *   B,C   SIM   S   (N*)

    Goal. Per current contract.

    Requirements. Per current contract.

    Performance Standard. Per current contract.

CACT-1103   4.0   *   B,C   SIM   S   (N*)

    Goal. Per current contract.

    Requirements. Per current contract.

    Performance Standard. Per current contract.

CACT-1104   4.0   *   B,C   SIM   S   (N*)

    Goal. Per current contract.

    Requirements. Per current contract.

    Performance Standard. Per current contract.

CACT-1105   4.0   365   B,C,R   SIM   S   (N*)

    Goal. Per current contract.

    Requirements. Per current contract.

    Performance Standard. Per current contract.

CACT-1106   4.0   365   B,C,R   SIM   S   (N*)

    Goal. Per current contract.

Requirements. Per current contract.

Performance Standard. Per current contract.

CACT-1107   4.0   365   B,C,R SIM   S   (N*)

Goal. Per current contract.

Requirements. Per current contract.

Performance Standard. Per current contract.

208. CORE SKILL PHASE

1. Core Skill Academic (ACAD).

   a. Purpose. Introduce the Pilots to the UC-35C/D.

   b. General. The Pilot should be CACT complete prior beginning this stage.

ACAD-2000   3.0   *   B,C,R 1 UC-35   A   D

   Goal. Introduce the UC-35 aircraft.

   Requirements.

      Brief. ADB, MEL/CDL, Chapter 29 Flight Crew Coordination, Pre-flight, Emergency Equipment, Egress Drill, Post Flight, M-Sharp, CP-Calc, Flight-planning, ORM, WX Brief, NOTAMS, Fuel Packet/Multi-use Card, OPARS, Short Field High Obstacle, CL-Calc. Discuss engine failure during critical phases of flight. Discuss Rapid decompression and time of useful consciousness. Discuss dual engine failure, ditching with two engines operative, single engine, and power off.

   Performance Standard. After introduction of above listed item, demonstrate understanding of each subject.

   External Syllabus Support. Static aircraft.

   Prerequisite. 1101-1107

ACAD-2001   3.0   *   B,C,R 1 UC-35   A   D

   Goal. Introduce the UC-35 avionics and navigation systems on a powered aircraft.

   Requirements. Demonstrate the power up, set up, and various functions of the FMS, radios and avionics.

   Performance Standard. Show proficiency in the use of all navigation equipment and radios.

   External Syllabus Support. Ground powered aircraft.

   Prerequisite. 2000

2. Familiarization (FAM)

   a. Purpose. Introduce Pilots to UC-35C/D FAM and CRM procedures.

   b. General

      (1) Basic, Conversion, and Refresher Pilots shall be trained and evaluated in the appropriate seat.

(2) Basic, Conversion, and Refresher Pilots shall complete the CACT prior to commencing flight training.

c. Crew Requirements. Shall be instructed/evaluated by an NI/ANI.

FAM-2100   2.0   *   B   1 UC-35   A   D

Goal. Introduce the UC-35 aircraft.

Requirements.

Brief: Stall warning/AOA, flying AOA, aircraft handling, Take-off abort, landing techniques/landing profile, engine limitations, electrical limitations, airframe limitations.

Flight: Practice - start, taxi, take off, climbs/descents, steep turns, slow flight, stabilized approach, landing.

Performance Standard. Demonstrate safe and proficient air work and show the ability to recognize deviation from Airline Transport Pilot (ATP) standards and work towards correction. Operate the aircraft according to the NFM, IFM, and FARs.

Prerequisite. 2000, 2001

FAM-2101   2.0   365   B,C,R 1 UC-35   A   D

Goal. Introduce expanded flight envelope.

Requirements.

Brief: Short Field/High Obstacles, Go-around Crew Coordination, Powerplant Malfunctions at V1, Crosswind Landing Techniques, Aerodynamic/Fuel/Autopilot Limitations. Discuss emergency evacuation of passengers and crew. Review emergency evacuation procedures.

Flight: Practice- Approach to Stall, Landing Pattern, Simulated Single-Engine Failure on Takeoff (NATOPS), Simulated Approach and Landing, Single-engine Go-Around, Two-Engine Go-Around, Emergency Descent, and Reduced Flap Landings (0/15)

Performance Standard. Demonstrate safe and proficient air work and show the ability to recognize deviation from Airline Transport Pilot (ATP) standards and work towards correction. Operate the aircraft according to the NFM, IFM and FARs.

External Syllabus Support. Approved working area or restricted area.

Prerequisite. 2100

3. Instruments (INST)

a. Purpose. Introduce Pilots to UC-35C/D Instrument procedures.

b. General. Basic, Conversion, and Refresher Pilots shall be trained and evaluated in the left seat.

INST-2200   2.0   365   B,C,R 1 UC-35   A   (N*)

Goal. Introduce instrument flying in the UC-35.

Requirements

Brief: Set-up of FMS,MFD,PFD. Discuss Jeppesen approach plates, NAVFIG, Giant Report, discuss TCASII warnings and conflict resolution maneuvers, IFR minimums.

Flight: ILS (coupled/non-coupled), PAR, Standby Gyro approach, Go-around, VOR holding, FMS holding.

Performance Standard. Demonstrate safe and proficient air work and show the ability to recognize deviation from Airline Transport Pilot (ATP) standards and work towards correction. Operate the aircraft according to the NFM, IFM and FARs.

INST-2201   2.0   365   B,C,R 1 UC-35 A   (N*)

Goal. Introduce expanded instrument flight and high altitude operations.

Requirements

Brief: RNAV/GPS, LNAV/MDA, LNAV/VNAV, VOR/TAC, ASR, B/C, GPS HOLDING, Instrument missed approach procedures, Standby Gyro Approach, NDB. Discuss volcanic ash hazards, recognition, and avoidance. Review pressurization system, rapid decompression. Discuss door seal warning, cabin door annunciation, emergency descent.

Flight: RNAV/GPS, LNAV/MDA, LNAV/VNAV, VOR/TAC, ASR, GPS holding, Instrument missed approach procedures, Standby Gyro Approach

Performance Standard. Demonstrate safe and proficient air work and show the ability to recognize deviation from Airline Transport Pilot (ATP) standards and work towards correction. Operate the aircraft according to the NFM, IFM and FARs.

4. Night Familiarization (NFAM)

   a. Purpose. Introduce Pilots to UC-35C/D Night Familiarization procedures.

   b. General. Basic, Conversion, and Refresher Pilots shall be trained and evaluated in the left seat.

NFAM-2300   1.5   180   B,C,R 1 UC-35 A   N*

Goal. Introduce night flying in the UC-35.

Requirements

Brief: Cockpit management and lighting, night emergency procedures to include; electrical fire and electrical failure, emergency lighting pack, and visual illusions. Discuss enhanced ground proximity warning system, controlled flight into terrain hazards, recognition, and CFIT escape maneuver.

Flight: Landing pattern, instrument approaches, simulated single engine failures, and go-around (one and two engines).

Performance Standard. Demonstrate safe and proficient air work and show the ability to recognize deviation from Airline Transport Pilot (ATP) standards and work towards correction. Operate the aircraft according to the NFM, IFM and FARs.

Prerequisite. 2101

5. Co-Pilot Responsibility (CP)

a. Purpose. Introduce UC-35C/D Co-Pilot responsibilities.

b. General. Basic, Conversion, and Refresher Pilots shall be trained and evaluated in the right seat.

CP-2400   2.0   *   B   1 UC-35 A   (N*)

Goal. Introduce right seat (pilot not flying) navigation, communication, and cockpit management duties. Introduce right seat approaches and landings.

Requirements

Brief: Aircraft servicing, NATOPS - Chapter 29 Flight Crew Coordination, ditching, weather radar, satellite phone, cabin ICS and audio capabilities, passenger/environmental comfort, passenger briefing/procedures, fuel planning (normal, long-range, over water). Discuss anti-icing system, airframe icing hazards.

Flight: Pilot not flying duties (normal procedures, normal checklists, simulated emergency procedures and abnormal checklists); Pilot Flying (approaches and landings).

Performance Standard. Demonstrate safe and proficient air work and effective cockpit management. Operate the aircraft according to the NFM, IFM and FARs.

CP-2401   2.0   60   B,C,R 1 UC-35 A   (N*)

Goal. Review right seat (pilot not flying) navigation, communication, and cockpit management duties. Review right seat approaches and landings.

Requirements.

Brief: Aircraft servicing, NATOPS - Chapter 29 Flight Crew Coordination, ditching, weather radar, satellite phone, cabin ICS and audio capabilities, passenger/environmental comfort, passenger briefing/procedures, fuel planning (normal, long-range, over water). Discuss windshear detection, avoidance, escape maneuver.

Flight: Review pilot not flying duties (normal procedures, normal checklists, simulated emergency procedures and abnormal checklists); Pilot Flying (approaches and landings).

Performance Standard. Demonstrate safe and proficient air work and effective cockpit management. Operate the aircraft according to the NFM, IFM and FARs.

Prerequisite. 2400

6. Familiarization Review (FAM REV)

a. Purpose. Review UC-35C/D FAM procedures.

b. General. Basic, Conversion, and Refresher Pilots shall be trained and evaluated in the left seat.

c. Crew Requirements. Shall be instructed/evaluated by an NI/ANI.

FAM REV-2500 2.0 * B 1 UC-35 A D

> Goal. Complete FAM Review.
>
> Requirement. Conduct an objective review of the Pilot's knowledge of mission planning, normal operating procedures (flight and ground), crew resource management, aircraft systems, performance criteria, emergency procedures, and debriefing. The focus is on normal and emergency procedures. Emphasis shall be placed on the aforementioned items with the addition of local course rules, unit SOP, and admin flight procedures. This review is the means to measure the Pilot's efficiency in the execution of normal operating procedures and reaction to emergencies and malfunctions. Review all previous requirements in preparation for upgrade/designation.
>
> Performance Standard. Demonstrate satisfactory knowledge of aircraft operating procedures and limitations. Demonstrate safe and proficient air work and show the ability to recognize deviation from Airline Transport Pilot (ATP) standards and work towards correction. Operate the aircraft according to the NFM, IFM and FARs.
>
> Prerequisite. 2101, 2201, 2300, 2401

209. MISSION SKILL PHASE (3000)

1. Operational Support Airlift

OSA-3100 2.0 60 B,R 1 UC-35 A (N*)

> Goal. Conduct an Operational Support Airlift (OSA) mission.
>
> Requirements.
>
> Brief: Mission and crew coordination, flight planning, weather, fuel requirements, weight and balance, aircraft performance factors, RON, passenger requirements, Scheduling agency coordination (JOSAC, MCB Japan), and emergency procedures.
>
> Flight: Conduct an OSA mission.
>
> Performance Standard. Demonstrate satisfactory knowledge of aircraft operating procedures and limitations. Demonstrate safe and proficient air work and show the ability to recognize deviation from Airline Transport Pilot (ATP) standards and work towards correction. Operate the aircraft according to the NFM, IFM and FARs.
>
> Prerequisite. 2000 Phase complete, 6100, 6101.

2. Air Logistics Support

ALS-3200 2.0 60 B,R 1 UC-35 A (N*)

> Goal. Conduct an Air Logistics Support (ALS) mission.
>
> Requirements.
>
> Brief: Mission and crew coordination, flight planning, weather, fuel requirements, weight and balance, aircraft performance factors, RON, Scheduling agency coordination (JOSAC, MCB Japan), cargo certification and handling, hazardous cargo considerations, and emergency procedures.

Flight: Conduct an ALS mission.

Performance Standard. Demonstrate satisfactory knowledge of aircraft operating procedures and limitations. Demonstrate safe and proficient air work and show the ability to recognize deviation from Airline Transport Pilot (ATP) standards and work towards correction. Operate the aircraft according to the NFM, IFM and FARs.

Prerequisite. 2000 Phase complete, 6100, 6101.

210. CORE PLUS PHASE (4000)

1. General

a. The Core Plus Phase consists of academics, skill, and mission training.

b. Core Plus training is defined as theater specific and/or low likelihood of occurrence training and should not be the focus of unit training.

c. The Pilot should be Core Skill complete prior to beginning the Core Plus Phase of training.

2. Core Plus Academics (ACAD)

ACAD-4000   2.0   *   B,R   CLRM

General. At the publishing date of this manual, the ASE academic period of instruction is under development by the Syllabus Sponsor (VMR Det Andrews) and it will be distributed to the UC-35 community once completed.

ACAD-4001   4.0   *   B,R   CLRM

Goal. Pilot under instruction is introduced to mission planning for extended over water and overseas operations.

Requirements. The PUI will be introduced to mission planning for a multiday, long range (1,200 nm) flight that should include the crossing of international airspace. The following tools commonly used for mission planning in the international environment should be introduced: Optimum Path Aircraft Routing System (OPARS), Aircraft/Personnel Automated Clearance System (APACS), Foreign Clearance Guide, Area Planning/General Planning (AP/GP), Giant Report/Global Decision Support System 2 (GDSS2) account, Naval Flight Information Group (NavFIG), Jeppesen View and the validation and use of Jeppesen terminal approach procedures, Universal Flight Planning software for oceanic remote operations, North Atlantic/Pacific Tracks message, North Atlantic/North Pacific Track Oceanic Checklist, North Atlantic Minimum Navigation Performance Specification Airspace Operations Manual, Equal Time Point (ETP)/Point of No Return (PNR), and Aircraft Flight Manual (AFM) Supplement 63. The following contingency and emergency operations will also be discussed: engine failure (drift down), loss of pressurization, lost communication, and weather avoidance/contingency operations in an RVSM and or non radar environment. Review ditching, post ditching aircraft evacuation procedures.

Performance Standard. Successful completion of the course of instruction.

3. Assault Support (AS)

AS-4100   1.5   *   B,R   UC-35   A   (N*)

General. At the publishing date of this manual, the AS flight is under development by the Syllabus Sponsor (VMR Det Andrews) and it will be distributed to the UC-35 community once completed.

Prerequisite. 4000

4. Expeditionary Shore-Based Operations (EXP)

EXP-4200   2.0   *   B,R   UC-35   A   (N*)

Goal. Conduct expeditionary shore-based operations.

Requirements. Conduct aviation operations from other than home field. This event should be logged any time an OAS-4100 or ALS-3200 is logged.

Performance Standard. Same as OAS-4100 or ALS-3200.

5. International Procedures (INT)

INT PROC-4300   3.0   *   B,R   UC-35   A   (N*)

Goal. Pilot under instruction performs extended range operations and alternates between left and right seats throughout the mission in order to demonstrate flight leadership from either seat.

Requirement. PUI shall demonstrate the ability to supervise preflight preparation and manage a crew and aircraft away from home station on an operational mission that should include a RON.

Brief: mission coordination, flight planning, weather, fuel planning, load computations, performance, CRM.

Conduct: PUI shall demonstrate flight leadership and Crew Resource Management by acting as the TAC during an operational mission that includes a RON. During the trip, the PUI shall conduct a two-engine instrument approach.

Performance Standard. Operate the aircraft according to the NFM IFM, FARs and ICAO procedures.

Prerequisite. 4001

INT PROC-4301   3.0   365   B,C,R   UC-35   A   D

Goal. Pilot Under Instruction conducts overwater navigation. Evaluation leg should be conducted with the PUI in the left or right seat.

Requirement. PUI to demonstrate the ability to manage a crew and aircraft on an extended, overwater flight under ICAO rules.

Brief: Mission coordination, crew briefing, ATFP briefing coordination, flight planning, weather brief, fuel planning, weight and balance, aircraft inspection, cargo inspection (as required), manifest inspection, trip aircraft clearance, foreign clearance guide review, survival gear inspection, fuel computations, performance, customs, and agriculture inspection.

Conduct: PUI to conduct overwater navigation in accordance with ICAO, FAR and NATOPS convention. The following contingency and emergency operations will also be discussed: engine failure (drift down), loss of pressurization, lost communication, and weather avoidance/contingency operations in an RVSM and or non radar environment. During the trip, the PUI shall conduct a two-engine instrument approach and landing from the left seat.

Performance Standard. Operate the aircraft according to the NFM IFM, FARs and ICAO procedures.

Prerequisite. 4001, 4300

211. INSTRUCTOR TRAINING (5000)

1. General. The Instructor Phase consists of four events leading to NATOPS Instructor and Assistant NATOPS Designations.

2. Instructor Under Training (IUT)

IUT-5100   1.5   *   B   E   1 UC-35   A   D

Goal. NI/ANI Training

Requirements

Introduce the IUT to the skills required to correct common student errors and prepare the IUT to conduct T&R syllabus and NATOPS/Instrument evaluation flights IAW Chap. 30 of the NATOPS Manual and OPNAV 3710.7.

Brief: Training Areas, Maneuver Descriptions, Operating Limitations, EP/Abnormals, Aeromedical Factors, Aerodynamics

Flight: Flight Planning, Weight & Balance, Performance Planning, Flight/Mission Briefing, Preflight/Postflight, Start, Taxi & Takeoff, Steep Turns, Slow Flight, Stalls, Fuel Management, Emergency Descent, Holding, Precision Approach, Wave Off(s), Non-Precision Approaches, Single Engine Work, Reduced Flap Landings, Contract Maintenance Procedures

Performance Standard. The IUT shall be evaluated on the ability to correctly brief the flight, demonstrate and introduce maneuvers in accordance with applicable directives, correct student deficiencies, conduct proper debrief and display appropriate subject matter expertise.

External Syllabus Support. Approved working area or restricted area.

Prerequisite. Qualified TAC, Standardization Board recommendation

IUT-5101   1.5   *   B   E   1 UC-35   A   D

Goal. NI/ANI Training

Requirements

Introduce the IUT to the skills required to correct common student errors and prepare the IUT to conduct T&R syllabus and

NATOPS/Instrument evaluation flights from the right seat IAW Chap. 30 of the NATOPS Manual and OPNAV 3710.7.

    Brief: Operating Limitations, EP/Abnormals, Aeromedical Factors, Aerodynamics

    Flight: Flight Planning, Weight & Balance, Performance Planning, Flight/Mission Briefing, Preflight/Postflight, Start, Taxi & Takeoff, Steep Turns, Slow Flight, Stalls, Fuel Management, Emergency Descent, Holding, Precision Approach, Wave Off(s), Non-Precision Approaches, Single Engine Work, Reduced Flap Landings, Contract Maintenance Procedures

Performance Standard. The IUT shall be evaluated on the ability to correctly brief the flight, demonstrate and introduce maneuvers in accordance with applicable directives, correct student deficiencies, conduct proper debrief and display appropriate subject matter expertise.

External Syllabus Support. Approved working area or restricted area.

Prerequisite. 5100

IUT-5102   1.5   *   B   E   1 UC-35 A   D

Goal. NI/ANI Training

Requirements

IUT shall refine the skills required to correct common student errors and prepare to conduct T&R syllabus and NATOPS/Instrument evaluation flights IAW Chap. 30 of the NATOPS Manual and OPNAV 3710.7.

    Brief: Operating Limitations, EP/Abnormals, Aeromedical Factors, Aerodynamics

    Flight: Flight Planning, Weight & Balance, Performance Planning, Flight/Mission Briefing, Preflight/Postflight, Start, Taxi & Takeoff, Steep Turns, Slow Flight, Stalls, Fuel Management, Emergency Descent, Holding, Precision Approach, Wave Off(s), Non-Precision Approaches, Single Engine Work, Reduced Flap Landings, Contract Maintenance Procedures

Performance Standard. The IUT shall be evaluated on the ability to correctly brief the flight, demonstrate and introduce maneuvers in accordance with applicable directives, correct student deficiencies, conduct proper debrief and display appropriate subject matter expertise.

External Syllabus Support. Approved working area or restricted area.

Prerequisite. 5101

IUT-5103   2.0   *   B,R   E   1 UC-35 A   D

Goal. NI/ANI Check

Requirements

IUT shall be evaluated on the skills required to correct common student errors and conduct T&R syllabus and NATOPS/Instrument evaluation flights from the right seat IAW Chap. 30 of the NATOPS Manual and OPNAV 3710.7. Flight should be completed in conjunction with a NATOPS/Instrument evaluation.

Brief: Operating Limitations, EP/Abnormals, Aeromedical Factors, Aerodynamics

Flight: Flight Planning, Weight & Balance, Performance Planning, Flight/Mission Briefing, Preflight/Postflight, Start, Taxi & Takeoff, Steep Turns, Slow Flight, Stalls, Fuel Management, Emergency Descent, Holding, Precision Approach, Wave Off(s), Non-Precision Approaches, Single Engine Work, Reduced Flap Landings, Contract Maintenance Procedures

Performance Standard. The IUT shall be evaluated on the ability to correctly brief the flight, demonstrate and introduce maneuvers in accordance with applicable directives, correct student deficiencies, conduct proper debrief and display appropriate subject matter expertise.

External Syllabus Support. Approved working area or restricted area.

Prerequisite. 5102

212. REQUIREMENTS, QUALIFICATIONS, DESIGNATIONS (RQD) PHASE (6000)

1. UC-35C/D RQD Academics

ACAD-6000   3.0   365   B,R   E   Open Book NATOPS Examination

Goal. The open book examination shall consist of, but not be limited to the question bank. The purpose of the open book examination is to evaluate the Pilot's knowledge of the appropriate publications and the aircraft.

Performance Standard. Achieve a minimum score of 3.5 on the open book examination.

ACAD-6001   1.0   365   B,R   E   Closed Book NATOPS Examination

Goal. The purpose of the closed book examination is to evaluate the Pilot's knowledge of normal/emergency procedures and aircraft limitations.

Performance Standard. Achieve a minimum score of 3.3 on the closed book examination.

Prerequisite. 6000

ACAD-6002   2.0   365   B,R   E   Oral NATOPS Examination

Goal. The oral examination shall consist of, but not be limited to the question bank. The instructor may draw upon their experience to ask questions of a direct and objective nature to evaluate the Pilot's knowledge of normal/emergency procedures, aircraft limitations, and performance.

Performance Standard. Achieve a minimum grade of qualified on the oral examination.

Prerequisite. 6000,6001

ACAD-6003   8.0   365   B,R   E   Instrument Ground School

Goal. The Instrument Ground School shall be an approved Commander Naval Air Forces (CNAF) syllabus.

Performance Standard. Achieve a minimum grade of qualified for Instrument Ground School.

ACAD-6004   1.0   365   B,R   E   Instrument Examination

Goal. Successful completion of the Instrument Examination.

Performance Standard. Achieve a minimum passing score on the Instrument Examination.

ACAD-6005   2.0   365   B,R   E   Instrument Oral Examination

Goal. The oral NATOPS instrument examination shall consist of, but not be limited to the question bank in addition to any subject listed for coverage in OPNAVINST 3710.7.

Performance Standard. Achieve a minimum grade of qualified on the oral NATOPS instrument examination.

Prerequisite. 6004

ACAD-6006   1.0   365   B,R   E   CRM BASIC

Goal. Introduce multi-piloted Crew Resource Management.

Requirement. This course of instruction is included in initial CACT.

ACAD-6007   1.0   365   B,R   E   CRM T/M/S

Goal. This course of instruction is under development by VMR Det Andrews and will be distributed to the UC-35 community once completed.

ACAD-6009   2.0   365   B,R   E   FCP Open Book Examination
Goal. The open book examination shall consist of 20 to 30 questions, including, but not limited to information from Chapter 10 of NATOPS. The purpose of the open book examination is to evaluate the Pilot's knowledge of FCF procedures and the aircraft systems and limitations.

Performance Standard. Achieve a minimum score of 3.5 on the open book examination.

ACAD-6010   1.0   30   B,R   E   Monthly EP Examination

Goal. Successfully complete the UC-35C/D Monthly Emergency Procedures Examination.

Requirement. Pass the Monthly Emergency Procedures Examination.

Performance Standard. Achieve a passing score on the Monthly Emergency Procedures Examination.

2. NATOPS Evaluation

NTPS-6100   2.0   365   B,R   E   S/A   1 UC-35   (N*)

   Goal. Complete annual NATOPS flight evaluation. Conduct an
   objective evaluation of the Pilot's knowledge of mission
   planning, normal operating procedures (flight and ground), crew
   resource management, aircraft systems, performance criteria,
   emergency procedures, and debriefing. The focus is on normal and
   emergency procedures. Emphasis shall be placed on the
   aforementioned items with the addition of local course rules,
   unit SOP, and admin flight procedures. The NATOPS evaluation is
   intended to evaluate compliance with NATOPS procedures. The
   NATOPS evaluation is the means to measure the Pilot's efficiency
   in the execution of normal operating procedures and reaction to
   emergencies and malfunctions. The NATOPS evaluation process
   should be as much a learning tool and/or experience as it is an
   evaluation.

   Requirement. Demonstrate comprehensive knowledge and
   understanding of NATOPS, unit SOP, and local course rules.

   Performance Standard. Executes flight and ground operations
   safely IAW OPNAV 3710.7, NATOPS and applicable manuals. Complies
   with unit SOP and local course rules.

   Prerequisite. Core Skill and Mission Skill Phase should be
   complete, ACPM 83XX Phase complete; 6000, 6001, 6002.

NTPS-6103   1.0   90   B,R   E   A   1 UC-35 (static)   (N*)

   Goal. Quarterly NATOPS static aircraft emergency procedures
   review.

   Requirement. This review should cover selected aircraft
   emergencies in a static aircraft. This event can be completed in
   conjunction with a flight. Demonstrate comprehensive knowledge
   and understanding of NATOPS emergencies.

   Performance Standard. Executes the review in accordance with
   NATOPS.

3. Instrument Evaluations

INST-6101   2.0   365   B,R   E   A/S   1 UC-35   (N*)

   Goal. Complete standard instrument flight evaluation. Following
   completion of the ground evaluation events, a standard instrument
   flight evaluation event shall be flown and completed with a grade
   of "Qualified." Conduct an objective evaluation of the airman's
   knowledge of flight planning, filing, briefing, and conduct of
   flight under normal operating conditions, emergency procedures,
   closing out flight plans, and debriefing.

   Requirement. Demonstrate comprehensive knowledge and
   understanding of instrument flight procedures, NATOPS, unit SOP,
   and local course rules.

   Performance Standard. Executes flight and ground operations
   safely IAW OPNAV 3710.7, NATOPS, NATOPS Instrument Flight Manual,
   and training rules.

Prerequisite. 6003, 6004, 6005

INST-6102   2.0   365   B,R   E   A/S 1 UC-35   (N*)

Goal. Complete special instrument flight evaluation. Following completion of the ground evaluation events, a special instrument flight evaluation event shall be flown and completed with a grade of "Qualified." Conduct an objective evaluation of the airman's knowledge of flight planning, filing, briefing, and conduct of flight under normal operating conditions, emergency procedures, closing out flight plans, and debriefing.

Requirement. Demonstrate comprehensive knowledge and understanding of instrument flight procedures, NATOPS, unit SOP, and local course rules.

Performance Standard. Executes flight and ground operations safely IAW OPNAV 3710.7, NATOPS, NATOPS Instrument Flight Manual, and training rules.

Prerequisite. Meets OPNAVINST 3710.7 Special Instrument requirements, recommended by Stan Board, 6003, 6004, 6005

4. Transport 3 Pilot (T3P)

T3P-6200   0.0   *   B   Transport 3 Pilot Tracking Code

Goal. Transport 3 Pilot tracking code. This code will be utilized when the Basic POI Pilot attains the hours in model (per UC-35 NATOPS) to be designated a T3P.

5. Transport 2 Pilot (T2P)

T2P-6300   1.5   365   B,R   E   1 UC-35 A   (N*)

Goal. Complete T2P flight evaluation. Conduct an objective evaluation of the Pilot's knowledge of mission planning, normal operating procedures (flight and ground), crew resource management, aircraft systems, performance criteria, emergency procedures, and debriefing. The focus is on normal and emergency procedures. Emphasis shall be placed on the aforementioned items with the addition of local course rules, unit SOP, and admin flight procedures. The T2P evaluation is intended to evaluate and measure the Pilot's ability to perform T2P functions and responsibilities.

Requirements. Demonstrate comprehensive knowledge and understanding of NATOPS, unit SOP, and local course rules.

Performance Standard. Executes flight and ground operations safely IAW OPNAV 3710.7, NATOPS and applicable manuals. Complies with unit SOP and local course rules.

Prerequisite. Core Skill and Mission Skill Phase should be complete, ACPM 83XX Phase complete; 6000, 6001, 6002, 6200.

T2P-6301   0.0   *   B,R   Transport 2 Pilot Tracking Code

Goal. Transport 2 Pilot tracking code. This code will be utilized when the B,C,or R POI Pilot attains the hours in model (per UC-35 NATOPS) to be designated a T2P.

6. <u>Transport Aircraft Commander (TAC)</u>

TAC-6400   1.5   *   B   E   1 UC-35 A   (N*)

    <u>Goal</u>. Complete TAC Mission Procedures Review. Pilot Under
    Instruction will plan, brief, execute, and debrief an OSA
    mission. Factors to review include, but are not limited to fuel
    planning, route planning, weather considerations, DV handling,
    weight & balance, aircraft performance, and JOSAC coordination.

    <u>Requirements</u>. Demonstrate comprehensive knowledge and
    understanding of NATOPS, unit SOP, and local course rules.

    <u>Performance Standard</u>. Executes flight and ground operations
    safely IAW OPNAV 3710.7, NATOPS and applicable manuals. Complies
    with unit SOP and local course rules.

    <u>Prerequisite</u>. 6301

TAC-6401   1.5   *   B   E   1 UC-35 A   D

    <u>Goal</u>. Complete TAC review flight. Conduct a review of mission
    planning, normal operating procedures (flight and ground), crew
    resource management, aircraft systems, performance criteria,
    emergency procedures, and debriefing. The focus is on normal and
    emergency procedures. Emphasis shall be placed on the
    aforementioned items with the addition of local course rules,
    unit SOP, and admin flight procedures. The TAC review is
    intended to review and assess the Pilot's ability to perform TAC
    functions and responsibilities.

    <u>Requirements</u>. Demonstrate comprehensive knowledge and
    understanding of NATOPS, unit SOP, and local course rules.

    <u>Performance Standard</u>. Executes flight and ground operations
    safely IAW OPNAV 3710.7, NATOPS and applicable manuals. Complies
    with unit SOP and local course rules.

    <u>Prerequisite</u>. 6400, 6008

TAC-6402   1.5 365 B,R   E   1 UC-35 A   (D)

    <u>Goal</u>. Complete TAC flight evaluation. Conduct an objective
    evaluation of the Pilot's knowledge of mission planning, normal
    operating procedures (flight and ground), crew resource
    management, aircraft systems, performance criteria, emergency
    procedures, and debriefing. The focus is on normal and emergency
    procedures. Emphasis shall be placed on the aforementioned items
    with the addition of local course rules, unit SOP, and admin
    flight procedures. The TAC evaluation is intended to evaluate
    and measure the Pilot's ability to perform TAC functions and
    responsibilities.

    <u>Requirements</u>. Demonstrate comprehensive knowledge and
    understanding of NATOPS, unit SOP, and local course rules.

    <u>Performance Standard</u>. Executes flight and ground operations
    safely IAW OPNAV 3710.7, NATOPS and applicable manuals. Complies
    with unit SOP and local course rules.

    <u>Prerequisite</u>. 6000, 6001, 6002, 6401

7. Functional Check Pilot (FCP)

FCP-6500   3.5   *   B   E   1 UC-35   A   D

    Goal. Instruct an NI/ANI on the safe and proper conduct of an FCF. This does not necessarily entail conducting an entire "A" profile in flight.

    Requirements. The flight shall consist of execution and/or discussion of all "A" profile functional check flight procedures from the left seat and be instructed by a qualified FCP Pilot.

        Brief: FCP Responsibilities, Briefing, Check Fight Profiles, Crew Coordination, Aircraft Limitations, Preflight, Start Procedures, Checklists, Stall/Spin Recovery, Airstart Procedures, Operating Limitations; Engine Performance, Pressurization, Bleed Air System, Aerodynamic, Avionic/Flight Instrument, Hydraulic System, and Electrical System Checks; Approach and Recovery, and Landing

        Flight: Preflight, Start Procedures, Checklists, Approach to Stalls, Airstart Procedures, Operating Limitations; Engine Performance, Pressurization, Bleed Air System, Aerodynamic, Avionic/Flight Instrument, Hydraulic System, and Electrical System Checks; Approach and Recovery, and Landing

    Performance Standard. Satisfactorily execute procedures per the NFM and IAW OPNAVINST 3710.7_.

    External Syllabus Support. Approved working area or restricted area.

    Prerequisite. 5103,6009,6402

FCP-6501   3.5   *   B,R   E   1 UC-35   A   D

    Goal. FCP Evaluation/Designation

    Requirements. The flight shall consist of execution and/or discussion of all "A" profile functional check flight procedures from the right seat and be evaluated by a qualified FCP Pilot.

        Brief: FCP Responsibilities, Briefing, Check Fight Profiles, Crew Coordination, Aircraft Limitations, Preflight, Start Procedures, Checklists, Stall/Spin Recovery, Airstart Procedures, Operating Limitations; Engine Performance, Pressurization, Bleed Air System, Aerodynamic, Avionic/Flight Instrument, Hydraulic System, and Electrical System Checks; Approach and Recovery, and Landing

        Flight: Preflight, Start Procedures, Checklists, Approach to Stalls, Airstart Procedures, Operating Limitations; Engine Performance, Pressurization, Bleed Air System, Aerodynamic, Avionic/Flight Instrument, Hydraulic System, and Electrical System Checks; Approach and Recovery, and Landing

    Performance Standard. Satisfactorily execute procedures per the NFM and IAW OPNAVINST 3710.7_.

    External Syllabus Support. Approved working area or restricted area.

    Prerequisite. FCP 6500

213. AVIATION CAREER PROGRESSION MODEL (8000)

1. Purpose

   a. To enhance professional understanding of Marine Aviation and the MAGTF and ensure individuals possess the requisite skills to fill battle command and battle staff positions in support of the ACE and the MAGTF in a joint environment. The focus of training in the Aviation Career Progression Model (ACPM) is on academic events in the following areas:

   Marine Air Command and Control System (MACCS)
   Aviation Ground Support
   Joint Air Operations
   ACE Battle Staff
   MAGTF
   Seabased Operations
   Combatant Commander Organizations

   b. All tactical T/M/S T&R manuals have ACPM training requirements embedded within the progressive training phases, including the flight leadership POI. If not already completed prior to assignment to VMR-1 or VMR Det (C-9, UC-35, C-12, or C-20), pilots assigned to an OSA platform shall complete ACPM training requirements as outlined per their original T/M/S MOS T&R manual. Refer to NAVMC 3500.14, Aviation T&R Program Manual, as a primary reference for ACPM training requirements.

2. General

   a. The ACPM is intended to be an integrated series of academic events contained within each phase of training. Accordingly, ACPM academic events are like any other academic event in that they serve as pre-requisites to selected flight events or stages. Additionally, several ACPM academic events are integrated as prerequisites for flight leadership syllabi.

   b. ACPM academic events, along with their identifying prerequisite association with other training phases/stages/events are listed below.

			VMR-1 VMR Det (UC-35)	
			ACPM TO UC-35 T&R MATRIX	
STAGE	EVENT NUMBER	CLASS	ACPM DESCRIPTION	PREREQUISITE TO (PHASE/STAGE/EVENT)
ACPM	8200	(U)	MACCS AGENCIES, FUNCTIONS AND CONTROL OF AIRCRAFT AND MISSLES	2000 PHASE
ACPM	8201	(U)	MWCS BRIEF	2000 PHASE
ACPM	8202	(U)	ACA AND AIRSPACE	2000 PHASE
ACPM	8210	(U)	AVIATION GROUND SUPPORT	2000 PHASE
ACPM	8230	(U)	ACE BATTLESTAFF	2000 PHASE
ACPM	8231	(U)	BATTLE COMMAND DISPLAY	2000 PHASE
ACPM	8240	(U)	SIX FUNCTIONS OF MARINE AVIATION	2000 PHASE
ACPM	8241	(U)	JTAR/ASR INTRODUCTION AND PRACTICAL APPLICATION CLASS	2000 PHASE
ACPM	8242	(U)	SITE COMMAND PRIMER	2000 PHASE
ACPM	8250	(U)	THEATER AIR GROUND SYSTEM (TAGS)	2000 PHASE
ACPM	8300	(U)	AIR DEFENSE	3000 PHASE
ACPM	8310	(U)	FORWARD ARMING AND REFUELING POINT (FARP) OPERATIONS	3000 PHASE
ACPM	8311	(U)	MARINE CORPS TACTICAL FUEL SYSTEMS	3000 PHASE
ACPM	8320	(U)	ACE BATTLE STAFF	3000 PHASE
ACPM	8321	(U)	JOINT AIR TASKING CYCLE PHASE 1: STRATEGY DEVELOPMENT	3000 PHASE
ACPM	8322	(U)	JOINT AIR TASKING CYCLE PHASE 2: TARGET DEVELOPMENT	3000 PHASE
ACPM	8323	(U)	JOINT AIR TASKING CYCLE PHASE 3: WEAPONING AND ALLOCATION	3000 PHASE
ACPM	8324	(U)	JOINT AIR TASKING CYCLE PHASE 4: JOINT ATO PRODUCTION	3000 PHASE
ACPM	8325	(U)	JOINT AIR TASKING CYCLE PHASE 5:	3000 PHASE
ACPM	8326	(U)	FORCE EXECUTION	3000 PHASE
ACPM	8340	(U)	JOINT AIR TASKING CYCLE PHASE 6: COMBAT ASSESMENT	3000 PHASE
ACPM	8350	(U)	INTEGRATING FIRES AND AIRSPACE WITHIN THE MAGTF	3000 PHASE
ACPM	8351	(U)	ESTABLISHING CONTROL ASHORE	3000 PHASE
ACPM	8630	(U)	TACRON ORGANIZATIONS AND FUNCTIONS	6000 PHASE
ACPM	8660	(U)	TACTICAL AIR COMMAND CENTER (TACC)	6000 PHASE
ACPM	8640	(U)	JOINT OPS INTRO	6000 PHASE
ACPM	8641	(U)	JOINT DATA NETWORK	6000 PHASE
ACPM	8620	(U)	ESG/CSG INTEGRATION	6000 PHASE

214. UC-35 T&R SYLLABUS MATRIX

UC-35 PILOT T&R MATRIX

STAGE	TRNG CODE	T&R DESCRIPTION	POI	DEVICE	# OF A/C	CON	RE FLY	# OF ACAD	ACAD TIME	# OF SIM	SIM TIME	# OF FLTS	FLT TIME	PREREQUISITE	NOTES	CHAINING	EVENT CONV
\multicolumn{18}{CORE SKILL INTRODUCTION TRAINING (1000 PHASE EVENTS)}
\multicolumn{18}{CORE SKILL ACADEMICS}
ACAD	1000	CACT SYSTEM INITIAL	B,C				*		55.0								
ACAD	1001	CACT SYSTEM REC	R				365		12.0								00
ACAD	1002	RVSM	B,C				*		3.0								
ACAD	1003	WEATHER RADAR	B,C,R				365		2.0								
ACAD	1004	CACT INTERNATIONAL PROCEDURES INITIAL	B,C				*		21.0								
ACAD	1005	CACT INTERNATIONAL PROCEDURES RECURRENT	R				365		8.0				1002			
		ACAD TOTAL						6	101.0	0	0.0	0	0.0				
\multicolumn{18}{CACT INITIAL SIMULATOR (CACT SIM)}
CACT SIM	1101	CACT SIM 1	B,C	S		(N*)	*				4.0						101
CACT SIM	1102	CACT SIM 2	B,C	S		(N*)	*				4.0						102
CACT SIM	1103	CACT SIM 3	B,C	S		(N*)	*				4.0						103
CACT SIM	1104	CACT SIM 4	B,C	S		(N*)	*				4.0						104
CACT SIM	1105	CACT SIM 5	B,C,R	S		(N*)	365				4.0						105
CACT SIM	1106	CACT SIM 6	B,C,R	S		(N*)	365				4.0						106
CACT SIM	1107	CACT SIM 7	B,C,R	S		(N*)	365				4.0						107
		CACT INT SIM TOTAL						.0	0.0	7	28.0	0	0.0				
\multicolumn{18}{CORE SKILL INTRODUCTION TRAINING (1000 PHASE EVENTS) TOTAL}	4	0.0	7	28.0	0	0.0				
\multicolumn{18}{CORE SKILL TRAINING (2000 PHASE EVENTS)}
\multicolumn{18}{CORE SKILL ACADEMICS (ACAD)}
ACAD	2000	INTRO LOCAL PROC	B,C,R	A	1	D	*		3.0					1101-1107			00
ACAD	2001	EMS PROCEDURES	B,C,R	A	1	D	*		3.0					2000			
		TOTAL ACAD STAGE						2	6.0	0	0.0	0	0.0				
\multicolumn{18}{FAMILIARIZATION (FAM)}
FAM	2100	INTRO UC-35 A/C	B	A	1	D	*						2.0	2000,2001			201
FAM	2101	INTRO EXPANDED ENVELOPE	B,C,R	A	1	D	365						2.0	2100			202

Enclosure (1)

UC-35 PILOT T&R MATRIX

STAGE	TRNG CODE	T&R DESCRIPTION	POI	DEVICE E	# OF A/C	CON	RE FLY	# OF ACAD	ACAD TIME	# OF SIM	SIM TIME	# OF FLTS	FLT TIME	PREREQUISITE	NOTES	CHAINING	EVENT CONV
		TOTAL FAM STAGE						0	0.0	0	0.0	2	4.0				
										INSTRUMENTS (INST)							
INST	2200	INTRO INST NAV	B,C,R	A	1	(N*)	365						2.0				210
INST	2201	HIGH ALT OPS	B,C,R	A	1	(N*)	365						2.0			2200	211
		TOTAL INST STAGE						0	0.0	0	0.0	2	4.0				
									NIGHT FAMILIARIZATION (NFAM)								
NFAM	2300	INTRO NIGHT OPS	B,C,R	A	1	N*	180					1	1.5	2101			220
		TOTAL NFAM STAGE						0	0.0	0	0.0	1	1.5				
									CO-PILOT RESPONSIBILITIES (CP)								
CP	2400	INTRO CP RESP	B	A	1	(N*)	*						2.0		RS		230
CP	2401	PRACTICE CP RESP	B,C,R	A	1	(N*)	60						2.0	2400	RS		231
		TOTAL CP STAGE						0	0.0	0	0.0	2	4.0				
									FAMILIARIZATION REVIEW (FAM REV)								
FAM REV	2500	PRAC FAM MANEUVERS	B	A	1	D	*						2.0	2101,2201,2300,2401		2101,2401	203
		TOTAL REV STAGE						0	0.0	0	0.0	1	2.0				
		CORE SKILL TRAINING (2000 PHASE EVENTS) TOTAL						2	6.0	0	0.0	8	14.0				
								MISSION SKILL TRAINING (3000 PHASE EVENTS)									
								OPERATIONAL SUPPORT AIRLIFT (OSA)									
OSA	3100	OSA	B,R	A	1	(N*)	60					1	2.0	2000 PHASE COMPLETE, 6100,6101	PAX	2201,2401,3200,2300~N	
		TOTAL OSA STAGE						0	0.0	0	0.0	1	2.0				
								AIR LOGISTICS SUPPORT (ALS)									
ALS	3200	ALS	B,R	A	1	(N*)	60					1	2.0	2000 PHASE COMPLETE, 6100,6101	CARGO	2201,2401,3100,2300~N	
		TOTAL ALS STAGE						0	0.0	0	0.0	1	2.0				
		TOTAL MISSION SKILL TRAINING (3000 PHASE EVENTS)						0	0.0	0	0.0	2	4.0				
								CORE PLUS TRAINING (4000 PHASE EVENTS)									
								CORE PLUS ACADEMICS									
ACAD	4000	ASE Academics, Tactical approaches & landings	B,R						2.0								

UC-35 PILOT T&R MATRIX

STAGE	TRNG CODE	T&R DESCRIPTION	POI	DEVICE E	# OF A/C	CON	RE FLY	# OF ACAD	ACAD TIME	# OF SIM	SIM TIME	# OF FLTS	FLT TIME	PREREQUISITE	NOTES	CHAINING	EVENT CONV
ACAD	4001	International Procedures	B,R					2	2.0								
		TOTAL ACAD STAGE						2	4.0	0		0					
ASSAULT SUPPORT (AS)																	
AS	4100	TACTICAL PROCEDURES	B,R	A	1	(N*)	*					1	1.5	4000	ASE	3100,3200	
		TOTAL AS STAGE						0	0.0	0	0.0	1	1.5				
EXPEDITIONARY SHORE-BASED OPERATIONS (EXP)																	
EXP	4200	EXP SHORE BASED OPS	B,R	A	1	(N*)	*					1	2.0			3100,3200	
		TOTAL EXP STAGE						0	0.0	0	0.0	1	2.0				
INTERNATIONAL PROCEDURES (INT)																	
INT PROC	4300	INTL OSA	B,R	A	1	(N*)	*					1	3.0	4001		3100,3200,2201,2401,2300~N,430 1	
INT PROC	4301	INTL ALS	B,R	A	2	(N*)	*					1	3.0	4001,4300		3100,3200,2201,2401,2300~N,430 0	
		TOTAL INT STAGE						0	0.0	0	0.0	2	6.0				
		CORE PLUS TRAINING (4000 PHASE EVENTS) TOTAL						2	4.0	0	0.0	4	9.5				
		2000, 3000, & 4000 PHASE TOTAL						8	10.0	7	28.0	14	27.5				
INSTRUCTOR TRAINING (500 PHASE EVENTS)																	
INSTRUCTOR UNDER TRAINING (IUT)																	
IUT	5100	INTRO FAM/INST MAN	B	E	A	1	D	*					1.5	TAC, STAN Board Rec			501
IUT	5101	PRAC FAM/INST MAN	B	E	A	1	D	*					1.5	5100	RS		502
IUT	5102	INSTRUCTIONAL TECHNIQUES	B	E	A	1	D	*					1.5	5101			503
IUT	5103	IUT EVAL	B,R	E	A	1	D	*					2.0	5102	RS		504
		TOTAL IUT STAGE						0	0.0	0	0.0	4	6.5				
		INSTRUCTOR TRAINING (5000 PHASE EVENTS) TOTAL						0	0.0	0	0.0	4	6.5				
REQUIREMENT, QUALIFICATIONS, AND DESIGNATIONS (RQD) (6000 PHASE)																	
RQD ACADEMICS (ACAD)																	
ACAD	6000	NATOPS Open Book Exam	B,R	E				365		3.0							
	6001	NATOPS Closed Book Exam	B,R	E				365		1.0				6000			
ACAD	6002	NATOPS Oral Exam	B,R	E				365		2.0				6000,6001			

2-28

Enclosure (1)

UC-35 PILOT T&R MATRIX

STAGE	TRNG CODE	T&R DESCRIPTION	POI	E	DEVICE	# OF A/C	CON	RE FLY	# OF ACAD	ACAD TIME	# SIM AC	SIM TIME	# OF FLTS	FLT TIME	PREREQUISITE	NOTES	CHAINING	EVENT CONV
ACAD	6003	Instrument Ground School	B,R	E						8.0								
ACAD	6004	Instrument Exam	B,R	E				365		1.0								
ACAD	6005	Instrument Oral Exam	B,R	E				365		2.0					6004			
ACAD	6006	CRM BASIC	B,R	E				365		1.0								
ACAD	6007	CRM T/M/S	B,R	E				365		1.0								
ACAD	6009	FCP RESPONSIBILITIES	B,R	E				365		2.0								
ACAD	6010	Monthly EP Exam	B,R	E				30		1.0								
		TOTAL ACAD STAGE							10	22.0	0	0.0	0	0.0				
		NATOPS																
NATOPS	6100	NATOPS Evaluation	B,R	E	S/A	1	(N*)	365				2.0		0.0	6000, 6001, 6002, see event			
NATOPS	6103	Quarterly EP Eval	B,R	E	A	1	(N*)	90		0.0		2.0	1	1.0				
		NATOPS TOTAL							0	0.0	1	2.0	1	1.0				
		INSTRUMENT (INST)																
INST	6101	Standard Instrument Eval	B,R	E	A/S	1	(N*)	365					1	2.0	6003, 6004, 6005			
INST	6102	Special Instrument Eval	B,R	E	A/S	1	(N*)	365						2.0	6003, 6004, 6005		6101	
		TOTAL INST STAGE							0	0.0	0	0.0	2	4.0				
		TRANSPORT 3 PILOT (T3P)																
T3P	6200	T3P DESIG TRACKING	B					*										250
		TOTAL T3P STAGE							0	0.0	0	0.0	0	0.0				
		TRANSPORT 2 PILOT (T2P)																
T2P	6300	T2P UPGRADE	B,R	E	A	1	D	365					1	1.5	6000, 6001, 6002, 6200			300
T2P	6301	T2P DESIG TRACKING	B,R					365										
		TOTAL T2P STAGE							0	0.0	0	0.0	0	0.0				300
		TRANSPORT AIRCRAFT COMMANDER (TAC)																
TAC	6400	Mission Proc Rev	B	E	A	1	(N*)	*					1	1.5	6301			400
TAC	6401	TAC REV	B	E	A	1	D	*					1	1.5	6400, 6008			401
TAC	6402	TAC EVAL	B,R	E	A	1	D	365					2	2.0	6000, 6001, 6002, 6401		6301	410
		TOTAL TAC STAGE							0	0.0	0	0.0	3	5.0				
		FUNCTIONAL CHECK PILOT (FCP)																

UC-35 PILOT T&R MATRIX

STAGE	TRNG CODE	T&R DESCRIPTION	POI	DEVICE E	DEVICE E	# OF A/C	CON	RE FLY	# OF ACAD	ACAD TIME	# OF SIM	SIM TIME	# OF FLTS	FLT TIME	PREREQUISITE	NOTES	CHAINING	EVENT CONV
FCP	6500	FCP REVIEW	B	E	A	1	D	*						3.5	5103, 6009, 6402			
FCP	6501	FCP EVAL	B,R	E	A	1	D	*						3.5	6500			
TOTAL FAC STAGE									0	0.0	0	0.0	2	7.0				

AVIATION CAREER PROGRESSION MODEL (ACPM)

STAGE	TRNG CODE	T&R DESCRIPTION	POI	DEVICE E	DEVICE E	# OF A/C	CON	RE FLY	# OF ACAD	ACAD TIME	# OF SIM	SIM TIME	# OF FLTS	FLT TIME	PREREQUISITE	NOTES	CHAINING	EVENT CONV
ACPM	8200	MACCS AGENCIES, FUNCTIONS AND CONTROL OF AIRCRAFT AND MISSLES						*		0.5					2000 PHASE			
ACPM	8201	MWCS BRIEF						*		0.5					2000 PHASE			
ACPM	8202	ACA AND AIRSPACE						*		0.8					2000 PHASE			
ACPM	8210	AVIATION GROUND SUPPORT						*		0.7					2000 PHASE			
ACPM	8230	ACE BATTLESTAFF						*		TBD					2000 PHASE			
ACPM	8231	BATTLE COMMAND DISPLAY						*		TBD					2000 PHASE			
ACPM	8240	SIX FUNCTIONS OF MARINE AVIATION						*		1.7					2000 PHASE			
ACPM	8241	JTAR/ASR INTRODUCTION AND PRACTICAL APPLICATION CLASS						*		1.3					2000 PHASE			
ACPM	8242	SITE COMMAND PRIMER						*		TBD					2000 PHASE			
ACPM	8250	THEATER AIR GROUND SYSTEM (TAGS)						*		0.9					2000 PHASE			
ACPM	8300	AIR DEFENSE						*		0.9					3000 PHASE			
ACPM	8310	FORWARD ARMING AND REFUELING POINT (FARP) OPERATIONS						*		0.8					3000 PHASE			
ACPM	8311	MARINE CORPS TACTICAL FUEL SYSTEMS						*		0.9					3000 PHASE			
ACPM	8320	ACE BATTLE STAFF						*		1.0					3000 PHASE			
ACPM	8321	JOINT AIR TASKING CYCLE PHASE 1: STRATEGY DEVELOPMENT						*		0.4					3000 PHASE			
ACPM	8322	JOINT AIR TASKING CYCLE PHASE 2: TARGET DEVELOPMENT						*		0.4					3000 PHASE			

UC-35 PILOT T&R MATRIX

STAGE	TRNG CODE	T&R DESCRIPTION	POI	DEVICE E	# OF A/C	CON	RE FLY	# OF ACAD	ACAD TIME	# OF SIM	SIM TIME	# OF FLTS	FLT TIME	PREREQUISITE	NOTES	CHAINING	EVENT CONV
ACPM	8323	JOINT AIR TASKING CYCLE PHASE 3: WEAPONING AND ALLOCATION					*		0.4					3000 PHASE			
ACPM	8324	JOINT AIR TASKING CYCLE PHASE 4: JOINT ATO PRODUCTION					*		0.4					3000 PHASE			
ACPM	8325	JOINT AIR TASKING CYCLE PHASE 5:					*		0.4					3000 PHASE			
ACPM	8326	FORCE EXECUTION					*		0.4					3000 PHASE			
ACPM	8340	JOINT AIR TASKING CYCLE PHASE 6: COMBAT ASSESSMENT					*		0.5					3000 PHASE			
ACPM	8350	INTEGRATING FIRES AND AIRSPACE WITHIN THE MAGTF					*		0.9					3000 PHASE			
ACPM	8351	ESTABLISHING CONTROL ASHORE					*		TBD					3000 PHASE			
ACPM	8630	TACRON ORGANIZATIONS AND FUNCTIONS					*		1.0					6000 PHASE			
ACPM	8660	TACTICAL AIR COMMAND CENTER (TACC)					*		0.5					6000 PHASE			
ACPM	8640	JOINT OPS INTRO					*		0.9					6000 PHASE			
ACPM	8641	JOINT DATA NETWORK					*		1.3					6000 PHASE			
ACPM	8620	ESG/CSG INTEGRATION					*		TBD					6000 PHASE			
		TOTAL ACPM STAGE						23	17.5	0	0.0	0	0.0				

Enclosure (1)

CHAPTER 3

UC-35C/D TRANSPORT AIRCREWMAN (TA)/6247

CHAPTER 3

UC-35 TRANSPORT AIRCREWMAN (TA)/6247

300. **UC-35 TRANSPORT AIRCREWMAN (TA)/6247 INDIVIDUAL TRAINING AND READINESS REQUIREMENTS.** This T&R syllabus is based on specific goals and performance standards designed to ensure individual proficiency in Core, Mission and Core Plus Skills. The goal of this chapter is to develop individual and unit war fighting capabilities.

301. **UC-35 TRANSPORT AIRCREWMAN TRAINING PROGRESSION MODEL.** This model represents the recommended training progression for the average UC-35 Transport Aircrewman crewmember. Units should use the model as a guide to generate individual training plans.

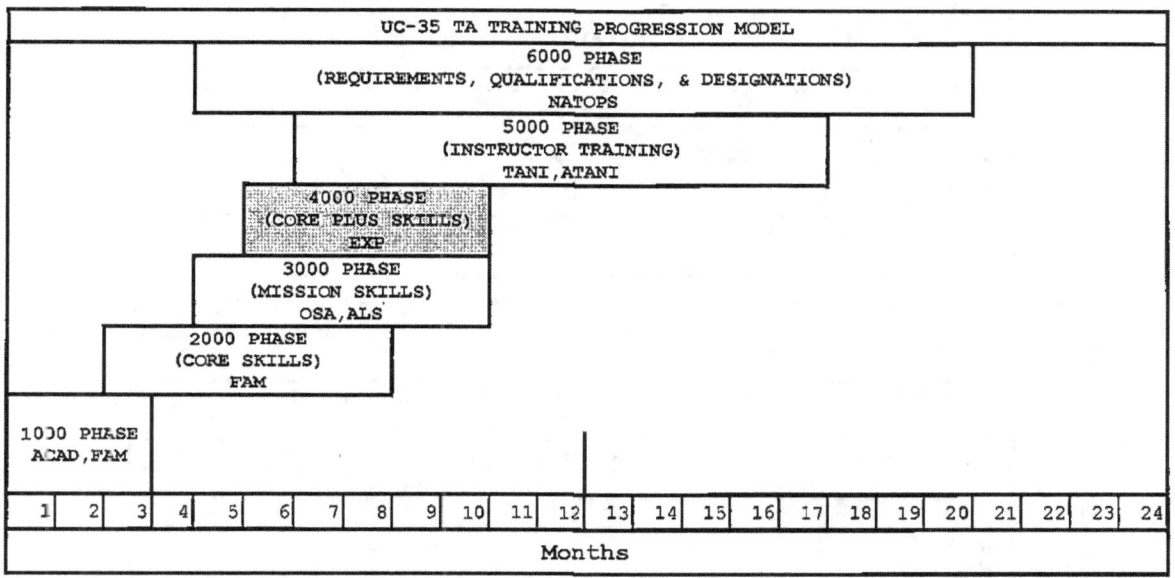

302. **INDIVIDUAL CORE SKILL PROFICIENCY (CSP) REQUIREMENTS.** A CSP crew consists of individuals representing each crew position who have achieved and currently maintain individual CSP. In order to be considered proficient in a Core Skill, an individual must attain and maintain proficiency in Core Skill events as delineated in the below paragraphs.

1. **Events Required to Attain Individual CSP.** To initially attain CSP in a Core Skill, an individual must simultaneously have a proficient status in all of the Core Skill (2000 Phase) T&R events listed in the table below for that Core Skill.

INDIVIDUAL CORE SKILL PROFICIENCY (CSP) ATTAIN TABLE
UC-35C/D Transport Aircrewman
FAM
2100R
2101R
Gray highlight & an R suffix on the event code = Refresher POI

2. **Events Required to Maintain Individual CSP.** To maintain CSP in a Core Skill, an individual must maintain proficiency in all 2000 phase T&R events listed for that Core Skill:

INDIVIDUAL CORE SKILL PROFICIENCY (CSP) MAINTAIN TABLE
UC-35C/D Transport Aircrewman
FAM
2101R
Gray highlight & an R suffix on the event code = Refresher POI

303. INDIVIDUAL MISSION SKILL PROFICIENCY (MSP) REQUIREMENTS. A MSP crew consists of individuals representing each crew position who have achieved and currently maintain Individual MSP. To be considered proficient in a Mission Skill, an individual must attain and maintain proficiency in Mission Skill events as delineated in the below paragraphs.

1. Events Required to Attain Individual MSP. To initially attain MSP in a Mission Skill, an individual must simultaneously have a proficient status in all 3000 phase T&R events listed for that Mission Skill:

INDIVIDUAL MISSION SKILL PROFICIENCY (MSP) ATTAIN TABLE	
UC-35C/D Transport Aircrewman	
T&R events required to Attain MSP (3000 Phase)	
OSA	ALS
3100R	3200R
Gray highlight & an R suffix on the event code = Refresher POI	

2. Events Required to Maintain Individual MSP. To maintain MSP in a Mission Skill, an individual must maintain proficiency in all 3000 phase T&R events listed for that Mission Skill:

INDIVIDUAL MISSION SKILL PROFICIENCY (MSP) MAINTAIN TABLE	
UC-35C/D Transport Aircrewman	
T&R events required to Maintain MSP (3000 Phase)	
OSA	ALS
3100R	3200R
Gray highlight & an R suffix on the event code = Refresher POI	

304. INDIVIDUAL CORE PLUS SKILL/MISSION PLUS SKILL PROFICIENCY REQUIREMENTS

1. Events Required to Attain Individual Proficiency in Core Plus Skills and Mission Plus Skills. Proficiency in Core Plus Skills/Mission Plus Skills is not required to obtain unit CSP. Training to Core Plus Skills/Mission Plus Skills is at the discretion of the unit commanding officer. To initially attain proficiency in a Core Plus Skill/Mission Plus Skill, an individual must simultaneously have a proficient status in all T&R events listed for that Core Plus Skill/Mission Plus Skill.

INDIVIDUAL CORE PLUS SKILL PROFICIENCY ATTAIN TABLE
UC-35C/D Transport Aircrewman
T&R events required to Attain Core Plus Proficiency (4000 Phase)
EXP
4200R
Gray highlight & an R suffix on the event code = Refresher POI

2. Events Required to Maintain Individual Proficiency in Core Plus Skills and Mission Plus Skills. To maintain proficiency in a Core Plus Skill/Mission Plus Skill, an individual must maintain proficiency in all T&R events listed in the table below for that Core Plus Skill Mission Plus Skill:

INDIVIDUAL CORE PLUS SKILL PROFICIENCY MAINTAIN TABLE UC-35C/D Transport Aircrewman
T&R events required to Maintain Core Plus Proficiency (4000 Phase)
EXP
4200R
Gray highlight & an R suffix on the event code = Refresher POI

305. CERTIFICATION, QUALIFICATION AND DESIGNATION TABLES. The tables below delineate T&R events required to be completed to attain proficiency, initial qualifications and designations. In addition to event requirements, all required stage lectures, briefs; squadron training, prerequisites, and other criteria shall be completed prior to completing final events. Certification, qualification and designation letters signed by the commanding officer shall be placed in Aircrew Performance Records (APR) and NATOPS. Loss of proficiency in all qualification events causes the associated qualification to be lost. Regaining a qualification requires completing all R-coded syllabus events associated with that qualification.

INDIVIDUAL DESIGNATION REQUIREMENTS UC-35C/D Transport Aircrewman	
Designation	Initial Event Designation Requirements
TA	6100
TANI	5000,5001,5002
ATANI	5000,5001,5002

INDIVIDUAL QUALIFICATION REQUIREMENTS UC-35C/D Transport Aircrewman	
Qualification	Initial Event Qualification Requirements
NATOPS	6000,6001,6002,6100
CRM	6003

306. PROGRAMS OF INSTRUCTION (POI)

1. General

   a. The time required to train a UC-35C/D Transport Aircrewman to completion of the Core Plus Phase is based off of flight hour requirements that are published in the UC-35 NATOPS manual. Assignment to a specific POI is determined by previous Aircrew experience. Transport Aircrewman Under Instruction (TAUI) without prior Naval Aircrew experience shall be assigned to the Basic (B) POI and shall continue to fly 2000 Phase level codes until the minimum flight hour requirement as delineated in NAVAIR 01-C35CAA-1 is met. TANI who were previously designated Naval Aircrew shall be assigned to the Basic (B) POI and may be designated as UC-35 TA upon successful completion of the Basic (B) POI. Those Aircrewman who were previously designated UC-35C/D TA's and are returning to a VMR shall be assigned to the Refresher (R) POI. When a crewmember completes a stage of training, that crewmember needs only to maintain proficiency in the (R) coded events for that stage to remain proficient.

b. All 1000 Phase level codes shall be instructed by a TANI. TAUI who are flying their 2000 Phase level codes to obtain their minimum flight hour requirement may fly with a qualified TA, TANI, or any qualified Pilot. 3000 Phase Level codes may be flown in place of 2000 level codes to obtain minimum flight hour requirements but shall be flown with a qualified TANI.

2. **Basic (B) POI.** Basic (B) Transport Aircrewman shall fly the entire syllabus.

WEEKS	COURSE	PERFORMING ACTIVITY
1-2	Core Skill Introduction Training	VMR Det
3-5	Core Skill Training	VMR Det
6-8	Mission Skill Training	VMR Det
9-10	Core Plus Training	VMR Det

3. **Refresher (R) POI.** Refresher Transport Aircrewman shall fly those events annotated with a R. Commanding officers/OICs will review the qualifications, previous experience, currency, and demonstrated ability of Refresher Transport Aircrewman with a view towards combining required flights.

WEEKS	COURSE	PERFORMING ACTIVITY
1-2	Core Skill Introduction Training	VMR Det
3-4	Core Skill Training	VMR Det
5-6	Mission Skill Training	VMR Det
7-8	Core Plus Training	VMR Det

307. **CORE SKILL INTRODCUTION PHASE (1000)**

1. **General**

   a. Core Skill Introduction training for the UC-35C/D is conducted at the squadron/unit.

   b. The purpose is to introduce Transport Aircrewman Under Instruction (TAUI) to the UC-35C/D. The focus shall be on Aircraft systems, handling, servicing, inspections and logistics

   c. All events in the Core Skill Introduction phase shall be evaluated and documented by a TANI. The Syllabus Sponsor shall ensure standardization of all TANIs.

   d. Event completion is predicated upon demonstrated proficiency. When an individual successfully accomplishes the requirements of an event per the performance standards, the individual should log completion of the event (enter the appropriate T&R code) in M-SHARP. When the event is entered into M-SHARP, the individual's proficiency date for that event is automatically updated to reflect the date the event was completed. When supervising individual events, unit instructors/leaders shall ensure that trainees demonstrate proficiency per T&R standards prior to logging successful event completion. Evaluating individual proficiency in an event normally requires both objective and subjective assessment. If an individual fails to accomplish the requirements of an event per the performance standards, the individual should not log that event and the proficiency status for that event remains unchanged. Times indicated for each event are for planning purposes only.

   e. **Environmental Conditions.** Transport Aircrewman shall fly events annotated with an N at least 30 minutes after official sunset. Events shall be flown in accordance with environmental conditions listed in the matrix below:

ENVIRONMENTAL CONDITIONS	
Code	Meaning
D	Shall be flown during hours of daylight: (by exception - there is no use of a symbol)
N*	Shall be flown during hours of darkness
(N*)	May be flown during hours of darkness

2. <u>Academic Ground School (ACAD)</u>

ACAD-1000   3.0   *   B   CLRM/1 UC35 (Static)

<u>Goal</u>. Introduce ground procedures, and aircraft systems.

<u>Requirements</u>. Discuss aircraft mission, qualification requirements, CRM, aircraft publications, flight publications, flight schedule, flight advisory, NAVFLIR, Logbooks, M-Sharp. Discuss UHF/SATCOM Operation, IFF Transponder Operation, HF Operation, ICS/Radio procedures. Discuss aircraft weight limitations; center of gravity limitations; weight and balance terms and definitions; fuel imbalance limitations and baggage loading.

<u>Performance Standard</u>. After introduction of above listed items, demonstrate understanding of each subject.

<u>External Syllabus Support</u>. Static aircraft with ground power unit.

ACAD-1001   2.0   *   B   CLRM/1 UC-35 (Static)

<u>Goal</u>. Introduce ground procedures, and aircraft systems.

<u>Requirements</u>. Introduce Flight line safety, aircraft danger areas. Introduce aircraft discrepancy book, contract maintenance personnel, general aircraft description, C/D differences, preflight, aircraft security, and aircraft parking. Introduce radio procedures, aircraft fueling, and engine oil servicing procedures. Introduce safety equipment, fire bottle location, survival equipment, ASE equipment and use, primary and emergency exit, O2 masks, egress, lavatory, coffee station, cabin preparation for flight, and seat operation. Review baggage loading.

<u>Performance Standard</u>. After introduction of above listed items, demonstrate understanding of each subject.

<u>External Syllabus Support</u>. Static aircraft with ground power unit.

<u>Prerequisite</u>. 1000

3. <u>Familiarization (FAM)</u>

   a. <u>Purpose</u>. Introduce Transport Aircrewman to UC-35C/D FAM and CRM procedures.

   b. <u>Crew Requirements</u>. Shall be instructed/evaluated by a TANI.

FAM-1100   1.5   *   B   1 UC-35 A   D

Goal. Introduce Operation of UC-35 aircraft.

Requirements. Introduce aircrew coordination/situational
awareness. Perform Weight and Balance; and aircrew brief.
Introduce normal and emergency checklist, flight packet,
communication during critical phases of flight, lookout doctrine
crew coordination, icing considerations, aircraft lighting, basic
cockpit familiarization, and duties during an emergency.
Introduce single-point and over the wing refueling procedures.
Introduce preflight and post-flight inspections.

Performance Standard. After introduction of above listed items,
demonstrate understanding of each subject.

Prerequisite. 1000, 1001

FAM-1101   1.5   *   B   1 UC-35 A   D

Goal. Familiarization with aircraft systems and emergency
procedures.

Requirements. Familiarize TAUI with aircrew
coordination/situational awareness. Perform Weight and Balance;
and aircrew brief. Familiarize normal and emergency checklist,
flight packet, communication during critical phases of flight,
lookout doctrine crew coordination, icing considerations,
aircraft lighting, basic cockpit operation, and duties during an
emergency. Familiarize single-point and over the wing refueling
procedures at civil airfields, Familiarize preflight and post-
flight inspections.

Performance Standard. After introduction of above listed items,
demonstrate understanding of each subject.

Prerequisite. 1100

FAM-1102   1.5   *   B,R   1 UC-35 A   N*

Goal. Familiarization with aircraft systems and emergency
procedures during night operations.

Requirements. Familiarize TAUI with nighttime aircrew
coordination/situational awareness. Perform Weight and Balance;
and aircrew brief. Familiarize TAUI with normal and emergency
checklist, flight packet, communication during critical phases of
flight, lookout doctrine crew coordination. Discuss night time
considerations, icing considerations, aircraft lighting, basic
cockpit operation, and duties during an emergency. Familiarize
TAUI with single-point and over the wing refueling procedures at
civil airfields, familiarize preflight and post-flight
inspections.

Performance Standard. After introduction of above listed items,
demonstrate understanding of each subject.

Prerequisite. 1101

308. CORE SKILL PHASE

1. General

a. Purpose. Familiarize the TAUI with the Operational Support Aircraft mission. The TAUI shall continue to fly these codes under actual or simulated conditions until minimum flight hour requirement is met IAW NAVAIR 01-C35CAA-1.

b. Crew Requirements. Shall be instructed/evaluated by a TANI.

2. Familiarization (FAM)

a. Purpose. Introduce Transport Aircrewman to UC-35C/D FAM and CRM procedures.

b. General. Basic, and Refresher Transport Aircrewman shall be trained and evaluated in their respective crew position.

c. Crew Requirements. Shall be instructed/evaluated by a TANI.

FAM-2100   1.5   *   B,R   1 UC-35   A   (N*)

Goal. Familiarization with Aircraft systems and radio operation.

Requirements. Familiarize TAUI in the operation of aircraft systems to include pressurization, communication, navigation, UHF and HF radio operation, and aircraft satellite phone. Practice normal procedures and simulated emergency procedures.

Performance Standard. After introduction of above listed items, demonstrate understanding and operation of each subject.

Prerequisite. 1102

FAM-2101   1.5   365   B,R   1 UC-35   A   D

Goal. Familiarization with DV passenger procedures.

Requirements. Familiarize TAUI with DV passenger procedures under simulated conditions. Discuss military appearance, customs and courtesies. DV Passenger comfort, baggage handling, passenger manifest, and passenger safety. Perform passenger brief.

Performance Standard. After introduction of above listed items, demonstrate understanding of each subject.

Prerequisite. 2100

309. MISSION SKILL PHASE (3000)

1. General

a. Purpose. Conduct Operational Support Airlift and Air Logistics Support missions as a Transport Aircrewman. TAUI may only fly these codes with a qualified Transport Aircrewmen. Initial codes shall be flown with a TANI/ATANI.

b. Crew Requirements. Shall be instructed/evaluated by a TANI.

2. Operational Support Airlift (OSA)

OSA-3100   1.5   60   B,R   1 UC-35 A   (N*)

    Goal. Conduct an Operational Support Airlift (OSA) Mission.

    Requirements. Conduct OSA mission: Crew coordination, fuel requirements, weight and balance, baggage handling, passenger comfort and safety, RON, normal and emergency procedures, passenger brief.

    Performance Standard. Conduct flight IAW NAVAIR 01-C35CAA-1. Assist pilots as required with all normal and emergency procedures.

    Prerequisite. 2101

3. Air Logistics Support ALS

ALS-3200   1.5   60   B,R   1 UC-35 A   (N*)

    Goal. Conduct an Air Logistics Support (ALS) Mission.

    Requirements. Conduct ALS mission: Crew coordination, fuel requirements, weight and balance, cargo certification and handling, hazardous cargo considerations, RON, normal and emergency procedures.

    Performance Standard. Conduct flight IAW NAVAIR 01-C35CAA-1. Assist pilots as required with all normal and emergency procedures.

    Prerequisite. 2101

310. CORE PLUS PHASE (4000)

1. General

    a. The Core Plus Phase consists of academics, skill, and mission training.

    b. Core Plus training is defined as theater specific and/or low likelihood of occurrence training and should not be the focus of unit training.

2. Expeditionary Shore-Based Operations (EXP)

EXP-4200   1.5   365   B,R   1 UC-35 A   (N*)

Goal. Conduct expeditionary shore-based operations.

    Requirements. Conduct aviation operations when deployed OCONUS. This event should be logged in conjunction with OAS-3100 or ALS-3200 when performed during contingency operations.

    Performance Standard. Conduct flight IAW NAVAIR 01-C35CAA-1 and Theatre specific SPINS.

    Prerequisite. 6100,6200

311. INSTRUCTOR TRAINING (5000)

1. General. The Instructor Phase consists of three events leading to the Transport Aircrewman NATOPS Instructor and Transport Aircrewman Assistant NATOPS Designations.

2. Instructor Under Training (IUT)

IUT-5000   1.5   *   B,R,   E   1 UC-35   A   (N*)

Goal. TA NATOPS Instructor Familiarization.

Requirements. Introduce the TANI under instruction (UI) to the skills required to correct common errors and prepare the TANI(UI) to conduct T&R syllabus and NATOPS evaluation flights IAW Chap 30 of NAVAIR 01-C35CAA-1. Discuss Instructional techniques and conducting a NATOPS Evaluation. Review all academic requirements, C/D differences. Review passenger procedures, night considerations, icing considerations, weight and balance, aircraft servicing and emergency procedures.

Performance Standard. After introduction of above listed item, demonstrate understanding of each subject.

Prerequisite. 6200

IUT-5001   1.5   *   B,R,   E   1 UC-35   A   (N*)

Goal. TA NATOPS Instructor Review.

Requirements. Review passenger manifest, passenger briefing, passenger procedures, DV procedures, hazardous cargo, aircraft handling, fueling, all weather operations and RON procedures. Discuss environmental system, pressurization system, oxygen system, anti-ice/de-ice systems and aircraft lighting. Practice preflight and postflight, checklists, all normal and emergency procedures, TA duties and responsibilities.

Performance Standard. Demonstrate satisfactory knowledge of passenger handling procedures and passenger brief. Assist pilots as required with all normal and emergency procedures.

Prerequisite. 5000

IUT-5002   1.5   365   B,R   E   1 UC-35   A   (N*)

Goal. TA NI/ANI designation evaluation flight.

Requirements. TANI(UI) is to brief and conduct a NATOPS evaluation on the TANI. TANI(UI) must show a thorough knowledge of all academic and flight requirements of a Transport Aircrewman and demonstrate the ability to instruct a student on the requirements.

Performance Standard. Demonstrate a thorough knowledge of and be able to effectively instruct all aircraft systems, limitations, normal and emergency procedures, and TA responsibilities.

Prerequisite. 5001

312. REQUIREMENTS, QUALIFICATIONS, DESIGNATIONS (RQD) PHASE (6000)

1. UC-35C/D RQD Academics (ACAD)

ACAD-6000   4.0 365 B,R   E   Open Book NATOPS Examination

> Goal. The open book examination shall consist of, but not be limited to the question bank found in the NAVAIR 01-C35CAA-1. The purpose of the open book examination is to evaluate the TA's knowledge of the appropriate publications and the aircraft.
>
> Performance Standard. Achieve a minimum score of 3.5 on the open book examination.

ACAD-6001   2.0 365 B,R   E   Closed Book NATOPS Examination

> Goal. The purpose of the closed book is to evaluate the TA's knowledge of normal and emergency procedures and aircraft limitations.
>
> Performance Standard. Achieve a minimum score of 3.3 on the closed book examination.
>
> Prerequisite. 6000

ACAD-6002   2.0 365 B,R   E   Oral NATOPS Examination

> Goal. The oral examination shall consist of, but not be limited to the question bank found in the NAVAIR 01-C35CAA-1. The instructor may draw upon their own experience to ask questions of a direct and objective nature to evaluate the TA's knowledge of normal and emergency procedures and aircraft limitations.
>
> Performance Standard. Achieve a minimum grade of qualified on the oral examination.
>
> Prerequisite. 6000,6001

ACAD-6003   2.0 365 B,R   E   CRM BASIC

> Goal. This course of instruction is under development by VMR Det Andrews and will be distributed to the UC-35 community once completed.
>
> Requirements.

ACAD-6004   1.0 30 B,R   E   Monthly EP Examination

> Goal. Successfully complete the UC-35C/D Monthly Emergency Procedures Examination.
>
> Requirement. Pass the Monthly Emergency Procedures Examination.
>
> Performance Standard. Achieve a passing score on the Monthly Emergency Procedures Examination.

2. NATOPS Evaluation

NTPS-6100   1.5   365   B,R   E   A   1 UC-35   (N*)

> Goal. Complete annual NATOPS flight evaluation. Conduct an evaluation of the TA's knowledge of mission and normal operating procedures (flight and ground), CRM, aircraft systems, emergency procedures.
>
> Requirements. Demonstrate a comprehensive knowledge and understanding of NATOPS, and SOP.
>
> Performance Standard. Achieve a minimum grade of qualified on the evaluation.
>
> Prerequisite. 6000,6001,6002,6003

3. Transport Aircrewman (TA)

TA-6200   0.0   *   B,R   Transport Aircrewman Tracking Code

> Goal. Transport Aircrewman designation tracking code. This code will be utilized when the (B) under instruction attains the hours required in model aircraft (as delineated in the NAVAIR 01-C35CAA-1) to be designated a TA.
>
> Requirements. Demonstrate a comprehensive knowledge and understanding of the TA's mission aboard the UC-35
>
> Performance Standard. This code will be flown in conjunction with the NATOPS 6200 for initial designation.
>
> Prerequisite. 6100, 3000 Phase complete

313. UC-35 TRANSPORT AIRCREWMAN (TA) T&R SYLLABUS MATRIX

UC-35 T&R MATRIX

STAGE	TRNG CODE	T&R DESCRIPTION	POI	DEVICE E	# OF A/C	CON	RE FLY	# OF ACAD	ACAD TIME	# OF SIM	SIM TIME	# OF FLTS	FLT TIME	PREREQUISITE	NOTES	CHAINING	EVENT CONV
CORE SKILL INTRODUCTION TRAINING (1000 PHASE EVENTS)																	
CORE SKILL ACADEMICS																	
ACAD	1000	GROUND PROCEDURES	B				*		3.0	0		0					100
ACAD	1001	AIRCRAFT SYSTEMS	B				*		3.0	0		0	0.0	1000			100
TOTAL CORE SKILL INTRODUCTION ACADEMICS								2	6.0	0	0.0	0	0.0				
FAMILIARIZATION (FAM)																	
FAM	1100	INTRO UC-35	B	A	1	D	*					1	1.5	1000,1001			101
FAM	1101	A/C SYSTEMS EPs	B	A	1	D	*					1	1.5	1100			101
FAM	1102	NIGHT FAM	B,R	A	1	N*	*					1	1.5	1101			102
TOTAL FAM STAGE								0	0.0	0	0.0	3	4.5				
CORE SKILL INTRODUCTION TRAINING (1000 PHASE EVENTS) TOTAL								2	6.0	0	0.0	3	4.5				
CORE SKILL TRAINING (2000 PHASE EVENTS)																	
FAMILIARIZATION (FAM)																	
FAM	2100	A/C SYSTEMS & RADIOS	B,R	A	1	(N*)	*					1	1.5	1102			200
FAM	2101	INTRO DV PROCEDURES	B,R	A	1	D	365					1	1.5	2100			201
TOTAL FAM STAGE								0	0.0	0	0.0	2	3.0				
CORE SKILL TRAINING (2000 PHASE EVENTS) TOTAL								0	0.0	0	0.0	2	3.0				
MISSION SKILL TRAINING (3000 PHASE EVENTS)																	
OPERATIONAL SUPPORT AIRLIFT (OSA)																	
OSA	3100	OSA	B,R	A	1	(N*)	60					1	1.5	2101	PAX	2101,3200	201
TOTAL OSA STAGE								0	0.0	0	0.0	1	1.5				
AIR LOGISTICS SUPPORT (ALS)																	
ALS	3200	ALS	B,R	A	1	(N*)	60					1	1.5	2101	CARGO	2101,3100	201
TOTAL ALS STAGE								0	0.0	0	0.0	1	1.5				
TOTAL MISSION SKILL TRAINING (3000 PHASE EVENTS)								0	0.0	0	0.0	2	3.0				
CORE PLUS TRAINING (4000 PHASE EVENTS)																	
EXPEDITIONARY SHORE-BASED OPERATIONS (EXP)																	
EXP	4200	EXP OPERATIONS	B,R	A	1	(N*)	365					1	1.5	6100,6200		3100,3200,2101	201
TOTAL EXP STAGE								0	0.0	0	0.0	1	1.5				
CORE PLUS TRAINING (4000 PHASE EVENTS) TOTAL								0	0.0	0	0.0	1	1.5				
2000, 3000, & 4000 PHASE TOTAL								0	0.0	0	0.0	5	7.5				
INSTRUCTOR TRAINING (500 PHASE EVENTS)																	
INSTRUCTOR UNDER TRAINING (IUT)																	
IUT	5000	INTRO FAM	B,R	E A	1	(N*)	*					1	1.5	6200			500
IUT	5001	INSTRUCTOR FAM	B,R	E A	1	(N*)	*					1	1.5	5000			501
IUT	5002	EVAL	B,R	E A	1	(N*)	*					1	1.5	5001			502
TOTAL IUT STAGE								0	0.0	0	0.0	3	4.5				

3-14

Enclosure (1)

UH-53E T&R MATRIX

STAGE	TRNG CODE	T&R DESCRIPTION	POI	DEVICE	# OF A/C	CON	RE FLY	# OF ACAD	ACAD TIME	# OF SIM	STM TIME	# OF FLTS	FLT TIME	PREREQUISITE	NOTES	CHAINING	EVENT CONV
INSTRUCTOR TRAINING (5000 PHASE EVENTS) TOTAL								0	0.0	0	0.0	3	4.5				
REQUIREMENT, QUALIFICATIONS, AND DESIGNATIONS (RQD) (6000 PHASE)																	
RQD ACADEMICS (ACAD)																	
ACAD	6000	NATOPS Open Book Exam	B,R	E			365		4.0								
ACAD	6001	NATOPS Closed Book	B,R	E			365		2.0					6000			
ACAD	6002	NATOPS Oral Exam	B,R	E			365		2.0					6000,6001			
ACAD	6003	CRM BASIC	B,R	E			365		2.0								
ACAD	6004	Monthly EP Exam	B,R	E			30		1.0								
TOTAL ACAD STAGE								5	11.0	0	0.0	0	0.0				
NATOPS																	
NATOPS	6100	NATOPS Evaluation	B,R	E	A	1	(N*) 365	0	0.0	0	0.0	1	1.5	6000,6001,6002,6003			400
NATOPS TOTAL								0	0.0	0	0.0	1	1.5				
TRANSPORT AIRCREWMAN (TA)																	
TA	6200	TA TRACKING CODE	B,R					0	0.0	0	0.0	0	0.0	6100, 3000 Phase Comp			
TOTAL T3P STAGE								0	0.0	0	0.0	0	0.0				400